D0338593

HILLSBORO PUBLIC LIBRARIES
Hillsboro, OR
Member of Washington County
COOPERATIVE LIBRARY SERVICES

FAITH & DOUBT

Resources by John Ortberg

An Ordinary Day with Jesus
(curriculum series, with Ruth Haley Barton)

Everybody's Normal Till You Get to Know Them
(book, audio, curriculum)

God Is Closer Than You Think
(book, audio, curriculum)

*If You Want to Walk on Water,
You've Got to Get Out of the Boat*
(book, audio, curriculum)

The Life You've Always Wanted
(book, audio, curriculum)

Living the God Life

Love Beyond Reason

Old Testament Challenge
(curriculum series, with Kevin and Sherry Harney)

When the Game Is Over, It All Goes Back in the Box
(book, audio, curriculum)

JOHN ORTBERG

FAITH

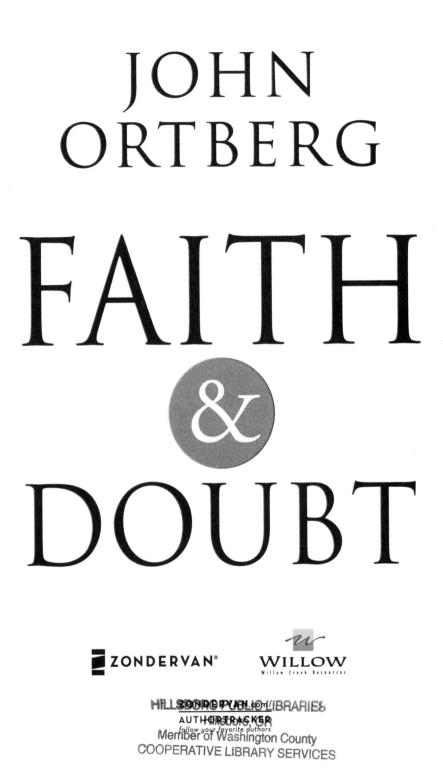

&

DOUBT

ZONDERVAN®

WILLOW
Willow Creek Resources

HILLSBORO PUBLIC LIBRARIES
Hillsboro, OR
Member of Washington County
COOPERATIVE LIBRARY SERVICES

ZONDERVAN.com/
AUTHORTRACKER
follow your favorite authors

Faith and Doubt
Copyright © 2008 by John Ortberg

This title is also available as a Zondervan ebook.
Visit www.zondervan.com/ebooks.

This title is also available in a Zondervan audio edition.
Visit www.zondervan.fm.

Requests for information should be addressed to:

Zondervan, *Grand Rapids, Michigan 49530*

Library of Congress Cataloging-in-Publication Data

Ortberg, John.
    Faith and doubt / John Ortberg.
        p.   cm.   39498836   1/09
    ISBN 978-0-310-25351-8 (hardcover, jacketed)
    1. Faith. I. Title.
    BT771.3.O78   2008
    234'.23 — dc22   2008013133

All Scripture quotations, unless otherwise indicated, are taken from the *Holy Bible: New International Version*®. NIV®. Copyright © 1973, 1978, 1984 by International Bible Society. Used by permission of Zondervan. All rights reserved.

Scripture quotations marked KJV are taken from the King James Version of the Bible.

Scripture quotations marked NASB are taken from the *New American Standard Bible*, © Copyright 1960, 1962, 1963, 1968, 1971, 1972, 1973, 1975, 1977, 1995 by The Lockman Foundation. Used by permission.

Scripture quotations marked TNIV are taken from the *Holy Bible, Today's New International Version*®. TNIV®. Copyright 2002, 2004 by International Bible Society. Used by permission of Zondervan. All rights reserved.

Internet addresses (websites, blogs, etc.) and telephone numbers printed in this book are offered as a resource to you. These are not intended in any way to be or imply an endorsement on the part of Zondervan, nor do we vouch for the content of these sites and numbers for the life of this book.

All rights reserved. No part of this publication may be reproduced, stored in a retrieval system, or transmitted in any form or by any means — electronic, mechanical, photocopy, recording, or any other — except for brief quotations in printed reviews, without the prior permission of the publisher.

Interior design by Beth Shagene

Printed in the United States of America

---

08 09 10 11 12 13 • 23 22 21 20 19 18 17 16 15 14 13 12 11 10 9 8 7 6 5 4 3 2 1

More than thirty years ago I and my best friends
sat at the feet of a redheaded, poor-joke-telling,
large-hearted, deeply sensitive, idea-loving,
self-effacing, life-changing Greek professor,

Gerald Hawthorne.

He led us into a larger and deeper world as an act of grace.
I learned more from him than I could ever say.
To him, this book is most gratefully dedicated.

CONTENTS

INTRODUCTION

I will tell you my secret: I have doubts.

I have spent my life studying and thinking and reading and teaching about God. I grew up in the church. I went to a faith-based college and then to a seminary. I walked the straight and narrow. I never sowed any wild oats.

And I have doubts.

I'll tell you more than that. There is a part of me that, after I die, if it all turns out to be true—the angels are singing, death is defeated, the roll is called up yonder and there I am—there is a part of me that will be surprised. What do you know? It's all true after all. I had my doubts.

Is it okay if we ask questions and consider objections and wonder out loud?

Is it okay if we don't pretend that everybody is split up into two camps: those who doubt and those who don't?

Is it possible—maybe even rational—to have faith in the presence of doubt?

Because I have faith too. And I have bet the farm.

And faith—like doubt—grows in unexpected places. A few months ago I received an email requesting a thousand copies of a book I had written. That was an unprecedented request from anyone besides my mother, so I was curious about the story.

It was from a young man named Kirk, a high-functioning corporate type, father of three young daughters with a brilliant future before him, who found out one year ago that he had ALS—Lou Gehrig's disease.

But Kirk was convinced that in the midst of tragedy faith was his only hope. And he decided to use his final months to invite the people he loved deepest to reflect on what mattered most.

The doctors told him he had two to five years to live, but he died in nine months. I write these words on a plane returning home from a dinner that his family sponsored, with hundreds of people, where we saw a videotape of Kirk, in a wheelchair, fighting for breath, speaking of his faith in God as the only force that could sustain him.

Kirk's dad drove me to the airport. He told me of difficulties in his life—how his mother had died when he was four, how now in his seventies he had lost his son. He told me of how he had once been an agnostic, and how he had come to believe.

I do not know why tragedy, which destroys faith in some people, gives birth to it in others. Suffering both raises unanswerable questions and tells us that our only hope must be a hope beyond ourselves.

There is a mystery to faith, as there is to life, that I don't fully understand.

This is a book with the not very catchy title Faith and Doubt, and the most important word in the title is the one in the middle.

Because most people I know are a mix of the two.

And it strikes me as arrogant when people on either side of the God-question write as if any reasonable person would agree with them because, of course, they wouldn't hold an opinion if it wasn't reasonable.

Introduction

Can I be faithful and still follow truth wherever it leads?

Is it possible that doubt might be one of those unwelcome guests of life that is sometimes, in the right circumstances, good for you?

I want to know....

ACKNOWLEDGMENTS

Writing a book, like having a child or buying a used car or getting out of bed in the morning, is always an act of faith. This one would not have happened without the encouragement and generosity of Menlo Park Presbyterian Church, which gives me both the time to write and stimulation to think.

I am also grateful to several folks who read the manuscript: to Chuck Bergstrom who doctored the text, to Christine Anderson who gave wonderful encouragement, to my daughter Laura who added ideas and readings and joy, to Mark Nelson who gave feedback that was scholarly and witty and accompanied by small cartoon illustrations that I wish could have been included in the text.

John Sloan is an editor who brings a deep love for the craft of writing to every project, and I am grateful for the growth he makes possible. Laura Weller gave careful labor to get every word right. And as the years pass I am increasingly grateful for getting to be part of a team and a community with Zondervan.

Not only did Nancy listen to the ideas behind this book while writing two of her own, but she is also my teacher about faith and trust and the joys of "strategic uncertainty."

Faith, Doubt, and Being Born

The deepest, the only theme of human history,
compared to which all others are of subordinate importance,
is the conflict of skepticism with faith.

Wolfgang von Goethe

One year, in the small cul-de-sac where my family lived in Illinois, three husbands in the four houses around us had heart attacks while still in their forties.

This was Illinois, where the state bird is sausage.

There were two immediate consequences. One was that my wife wanted to know the details of our life insurance policy. The other was that everybody wanted to know what lies on the other side when the heart stops beating. Questions about God and heaven and meaning and death ceased to be academic.

And it struck me, in that year, how deeply both faith and doubt are part of my life. We often think of them as opposites. Many books argue for one or the other. But while in some respects they are enemies, in other ways they are surprisingly alike: both are

15

concerned with ultimate issues; both pop up unasked for at unexpected moments; both are necessary.

I must have truth. Therefore I doubt. If I did not doubt, I'd be just another one of those suckers P. T. Barnum was so grateful get born once a minute; I'd fall for every carnival sideshow delusion that comes along. And I scorn delusion.

I must have hope. Therefore I believe. If I did not believe, I would cave in to despair. And I dread despair.

In addition to believing and doubting, there is choosing. I must decide which road I will follow. I must place my bet.

Why I Believe

If you were to ask me why I believe in God, I suppose I would tell you a story about a baby. She was not the beginning of my faith in God, but she was a new chapter of it. I did not know that when a baby came into my world she would bring God with her.

When we found out baby number one was on the way, Nancy and I went through a Lamaze class together. To spare the moms-to-be anxiety, the instructors did not use the word *pain*. They spoke of *discomfort*, as in "When the baby is born, you may experience some discomfort."

On our second anniversary, Nancy began what would be twelve hours of labor. (All of our kids arrived on notable occasions, none more so than Johnny. He popped into the world on February 2, prompting the doctor to tell us that if he saw his shadow, he would go back inside and Nancy would have six more weeks of pregnancy.)

Laura's body was unusually positioned inside Nancy (the phrase the nurses used was "sunny-side up") so that the hardest part of her head was pressing against Nancy's spine. Each contraction was excruciating. The worst moment came after eleven hours and several doses of Pitocin to heighten the contractions. The doctor, with a single hand, wrenched the baby 180 degrees around inside my wife's body. Nancy let out a scream I will never forget. I knew I had to say something. "Honey—are you experiencing some discomfort?"

They finally had to use a vacuum cleaner with a special attachment to get the baby out. (The Lamaze people had warned us this procedure might make the cranium look pointed, but it would only be temporary.)

Suddenly the pain was over, and we held this little conehead in our arms and were totally unprepared for the world we had entered. Nancy, who had never been particularly attracted to anybody else's children, held the baby and looked around the room like a mother tigress. "I would *kill* for this baby."

I pointed out that I thought most mothers would say that they would *die* for their children.

"*Die?* Why would I want to die? If I died for her, then I couldn't be with her. I'd *kill* for her." And she looked around the room, clearly hoping someone would give her the chance to show she wasn't bluffing.

I took the baby from her and was overwhelmed by the wonder and mystery of the presence of a human person. Not just the mechanics of her body—though they were amazing. Not just my sudden love for this being—though it was a flood tide. What overwhelmed me was being in the presence of a new *soul*.

> Not just the mechanics of her body—though they were amazing. Not just my sudden love for this being—though it was a flood tide. What overwhelmed me was being in the presence of a new soul.

"I can't believe that there is a live, flesh-and-blood, immortal being in this room who didn't used to exist. She will grow up—and we'll watch her. She'll become a woman. And then one day she'll grow old. This red hair will turn to gray and then to white; this same skin that is so pink and smooth right now will be mottled and wrinkled, and she'll be an old lady sitting in a rocking chair—and it will be *this same person*," I said to Nancy.

"Yes," she said. "And I'd kill for the old lady too."

We propped that tiny body with towels and blankets in the car seat of my old VW Super Beetle to take her home. I drove like I was transporting nitroglycerin. I crawled along the freeway in the slow lane, hazard lights flashing, doing twenty-five miles per hour, ticking off motorists from Northridge to Pasadena. How do you travel carefully enough to protect a new soul?

When I held Laura, I found myself incapable of believing that she was an accident. I found myself incapable of believing that the universe was a random chaotic machine that did not care whether I loved her or hated her. I don't mean that I had a group of arguments for her having a soul and I believed those arguments. I don't mean this conviction is always present in my mind with equal force. It's not.

I mean the conviction welled up inside me and I could not get away from it. I could not look at Laura and believe otherwise. I could not hold her without saying thank you to Someone for her. I could not think of her future without praying for Someone more powerful and wiser than me to watch over her. When she arrived, she brought along with her a world that was meant to be a home for persons. A God-breathed world.

Every child is a testimony to God's desire that the world go on. Elie Wiesel, the Holocaust survivor who doubts sometimes, has written that the reason so many babies keep being born is that God loves stories.

Why I Doubt

On the other hand, if you were to ask me why I doubt, I suppose I would tell you a story about a baby as well. A couple whom I have known for a long time had a beautiful little daughter. She was the kind of child who was so beautiful that people would stop them on the street to comment on her beauty. They were the kind of parents you would hope every child might have.

They had a pool in their backyard.

One summer day it was so nice outside that the mom set up the playpen in the backyard so that her daughter could enjoy the day. The phone rang, and her daughter was in the playpen, so she went in to answer the phone. Her daughter tugged on the wall of that playpen, and the hinge that held the side up gave way. It didn't have to. God could have stopped it. God could have reached down from heaven and straightened it out and kept that playpen up. He didn't. The hinge gave way, and the side came down, and the baby crawled out, and heaven was silent.

When that mom came outside, she saw the beautiful little body of her beloved daughter at the bottom of that pool. It was the beginning of a pain that no words could name. She would have died if doing so could have changed that one moment. But she could not. She would have to live. The memory of how old her daughter would be would have to haunt her every birthday and every Christmas and on the day she would have graduated from high school. That mom would live with the emptiness, the guilt, the blame, and the aloneness.

When that little baby left this world, she left behind a world that was God-silent.

Dostoyevsky, who was a believer, wrote that the "death of a single infant calls into question the existence of God." But of course death has not restricted itself to just one infant. Elie Wiesel tells of his first night in a concentration camp and seeing a wagonload of babies driven up. They were unloaded and thrown into a ditch of fire. "Never shall I forget ... the first night in camp, which has turned my life into one long night, seven times cursed and seven times sealed. ... Never shall I forget those moments that murdered my God and my soul and turned my dreams to dust. Never shall I forget these things, even if I am condemned to live as long as God Himself. Never."

This is our world. I don't know all the right responses to resolve these issues, but I know some of the wrong ones.

Wanting to Believe

When people of faith are not willing to sit quietly sometimes and let doubt make its case, bad things can happen.

Sometimes people of faith can be glib. Sometimes they respond with bad answers.

Sometimes preachers add enormous pain by telling people they have brought suffering on themselves by sinning. Sometimes they tell people they have not been delivered because they do not have enough faith.

Sometimes people want to believe but find they can't.

I think of a man who prayed for his alcoholic father for twenty years—but his father never changed.

I think of a woman who prayed for a mentally ill sister who committed suicide.

I think of a brilliant young girl who was neglected by her mom, abandoned by her dad, and molested by her uncle. She was an atheist at age eleven and then through a group of friends became a Christian. But she was tormented with sexual addictions all through her teenage years. She began to be troubled by the thought that some people were condemned to hell just because they belonged to a different religion. She kept asking God to help her; she kept asking for answers, but nothing seemed to change.

> *When people of faith are not willing to sit quietly sometimes and let doubt make its case, bad things can happen.*

I think of a letter I received recently:

> *How can I believe a Jewish friend who is devoted to God and hears him better than I do will go to hell and I will go to heaven even though I'm not as good as he is, just because I am a Christian and he is not? Will the real God and creator of the universe stand up?*
>
> *The God I used to believe in was very easy to hear and follow. Now I'm in the dark, and he feels like a stranger. I'm praying but am getting nervous that he won't answer because I now have so little faith . . . not even the size of a grain of mustard seed.*

Philosopher André Comte-Sponville writes poignantly about the beauty of humility: "Humility may be the most religious of virtues. How one longs to kneel down in churches!" But he said he could not bring himself to do this because he would have to believe that God created him, and human beings seem to him too wretched to permit that possibility. "To believe in God would be a sin of pride."

Wanting to Doubt

Sometimes people want *not* to believe. A number of recent bestsellers by professional doubters are part of what is being called the New Atheism, a kind of reverse evangelism. They are written by people who are quite certain that God does not exist, and in some cases they are mad at him for not existing. Philosopher Daniel C. Dennett wrote *Breaking the Spell* to argue that religious faith has been protected by the idea that it is holy or sacred. He says a little critical thinking that would reveal it to be nonsensical would "break the spell."

Noted author Sam Harris writes that the only difference between believing *in* Jesus and thinking that you *are* Jesus is the number of people involved in each category. "We have names for

people who have many beliefs for which there are no rational justification. When their beliefs are extremely common, we call them
'religious.' Otherwise, they are likely to be called 'mad, psychotic,
or delusional.' While religious people are not generally mad, their
core beliefs absolutely are."

British journalist Christopher Hitchens has written *God Is Not
Great: How Religion Poisons Everything*. The title pretty much tells
where the book heads.

Oxford biologist Richard Dawkins says in *The God Delusion*:
"The God of the Old Testament is arguably the most unpleasant
character in all of fiction. Jealous and proud of it, a petty, un-
just, unforgiving control freak, a vindictive, bloodthirsty ethnic
cleanser, a misogynistic, homophobic, racist, infanticidal, geno-
cidal, filicidal, pestilential, megalomaniacal ..." He gets hostile
after that.

The current popularity of such books may have been sparked,
chronologically at least, by Daniel Brown's *The Da Vinci Code*.
With this book Brown sought to under-
mine almost all the historical basis for
orthodox Christianity, although what
gets presented as history in *The Da Vinci
Code* is hotly contested by scholars of all
stripes. (A historian friend of mine said,
perhaps a little unkindly, that *The Da
Vinci Code* is the only book after which
you've read it, you're dumber than you
were before you started.)

> Ever since what
> was modestly called
> the Enlightenment,
> people have been
> predicting the demise
> of faith in God. I want
> to listen to doubters
> and not just argue
> with them.

Ever since what was modestly called
the Enlightenment, people have been
predicting the demise of faith in God. I want to listen to doubters
and not just argue with them, partly because deep down I have
doubts enough of my own, and partly because when I'm just trying
to win arguments, I turn into Dan Ackroyd debating Jane Curtain

in an old *Saturday Night Live* sketch: "Jane, you ignorant ..." Nobody wants to be around me then. Not even me.

I do not like books by believers or doubters that make it sound like the question of God is simple, that anyone with half a brain will agree with them, that people in the other camp are foolish and evil. I have read and known too many people who don't believe in God who are better and wiser than me. But I do not think the professional doubters will make faith go away. The predictors keep dying, and faith keeps spreading.

Doubt and Faith in Every Soul

Because old Mother Nature is a dysfunctional parent who keeps sending us mixed messages, we need both faith and doubt. The birth of every infant whispers of a God who loves stories; the death of every infant calls his existence into question. Writer Michael Novak says that doubt is not so much a dividing line that separates people into different camps as it is a razor's edge that runs through every soul. Many believers tend to think doubters are given over to meaninglessness, moral confusion, and despair. Many doubters assume believers are nonthinking, dogmatic, judgmental moralizers. But the reality is, we all have believing and doubting inside us. For "we all have the same contradictory information to work with."

Perhaps great believers and great doubters are more like each other than either group is like the great mass of relatively disinterested middle-grounders. Both are preoccupied with understanding the nature of the universe. Both agree that this is, after all, the great question. Most doubters know the discomfort of uncertainty. An agnostic writer for *Wired* magazine reviewed the works of the New Atheists and wrote of his envy of their certainty, his attraction to declaring himself an atheist rather than simply an agnostic. In the end, though, he could not join their ranks, because, he said, "I might be wrong." Another prominent scientist writes, "I have wavered between the comfortable certainty of atheism and the gnawing doubts of agnosticism my entire life."

But most believers know uncertainty as well. Billy Graham, an old man near ninety, when asked if he believes that after he dies he will hear God say to him, "Well done, good and faithful servant," pauses and says after a surprising inner struggle, "I hope so." Martin Luther, the champion of justification by faith, was approached for help by an elderly woman troubled by doubt. "Tell me," he asked her, "when you recite the creeds—do you believe them?" "Yes, most certainly." "Then go in peace," the reformer said. "You believe more and better than I do." Elie Wiesel, when asked to describe his faith, uses the adjective *wounded*. "My tradition teaches that no heart is as whole as a broken heart, and I would say that no faith is as solid as a wounded faith." I believe. And I doubt. The razor's edge runs through me as well.

> One of the paradoxes of faith and doubt is that it is the ultimate intellectual challenge, yet simple and uneducated people may live with great wisdom and PhDs may choose folly.

Sometimes I get frustrated and feel that if I were only smarter I could figure the whole God-issue out beyond doubts. I feel as if I'm back in school taking a math test with the really hard question about one train leaving Cleveland going twenty-five miles an hour and one leaving Pittsburgh doing thirty and when do they pass each other, and that the proof about God has to be out there if I just had more time or could find the right book. I'm tempted to think that doubt is merely a problem of intellect. But making the right choices about faith—like making good choices for life in general—does not seem to rest primarily on IQ. Smart people mess up as easily as the rest of us.

Three men are in a plane: a pilot, a Boy Scout, and the world's smartest man. The engine fails, the plane is going down, and there are only two parachutes. The smart man grabs one. "I'm sorry about this," he says, "but I'm the smartest man in the world; I have a responsibility to the planet," and he jumps out of the plane. The pilot turns to the Boy Scout and speaks of how he has lived a long, full life and how the Boy Scout has his whole life in front of him. He tells the Boy Scout to take the last parachute and live. "Relax, Captain," the Boy Scout says. "The world's smartest man just jumped out of the plane with my backpack."

Our world is full of smart people jumping out of planes with backpacks. One of the paradoxes of faith and doubt is that it is the ultimate intellectual challenge, yet simple and uneducated people may live with great wisdom and PhDs may choose folly.

One thing is for sure: sooner or later the plane is going down. We all are on the same plane. Smart guys and Boys Scouts alike: everybody has to jump. Everybody has to choose a parachute. No one will know who chose wisely until after they jump.

Nicholas Wolterstorff, a brilliant philosopher at Yale, is the father of a son who died at age twenty-five climbing a mountain. Wolterstorff is also a believer who asks questions. He writes of how some people try to explain the problem of death by saying God is its agent, with a not-so-subtle reference to his son: "You have lived out the years I've planned for you, so I'll just shake the mountain a bit. All of you there, I'll send some starlings into the engine of your plane. And as for you there, a stroke while running will do nicely."

Others, like Rabbi Harold Kushner, try to explain suffering by saying God too is pained by death but cannot do anything about it. (Elie Wiesel once said in response to Kushner, "If that's who God is, he should resign and let someone competent take over.")

Wolterstorff writes as a believer who still has unanswered questions.

> I cannot fit it all together by saying, "He did it," but neither can I do so by saying, "There was nothing he could do about

it." I cannot fit it together at all.... I have read the theodicies produced to justify the ways of God to man. I find them unconvincing. To the most agonized question I have ever asked I do not know the answer. I do not know why God would watch him fall. I do not know why God would watch me wounded. I cannot even guess. My wound is an unanswered question. The wounds of all humanity are an unanswered question.

So it goes for those of us who live in a cul-de-sac, where babies are brought home from the hospital and watched over, where hearts stop and feet slip, where we wonder if there is a hidden road that leads somewhere.

We believe and we doubt. Believing and doubting share the same inevitability, but they are not equal. They cannot lay the same claim on our allegiance. They do not share the same power.

If there are places beyond the cul-de-sac, doubt cannot take us there.

WHY BOTHER?

> Faith is a free surrender and a joyous wager on the unseen,
> unknown, untested goodness of God.
>
> **MARTIN LUTHER**

When Smart People Disagree

Have you ever considered how many different ideas about faith, religion, and God exist among the human race?

There are Christians. There are Hindus. There are Muslims —Shiites and Sunnis. There are Confucianists, Shintoists, Buddhists, Bahais, Rostafarians, atheists, agnostics, nihilists, humanists, deists, pantheists, New Agers, witches, wizards, and satanists. There is a group online who claims to believe in a Flying Spaghetti Monster. There are certain followers of Jainism who believe there are over three hundred thousand gods. There are Unitarians who, Bertrand Russell said, believe there is *at most* one God.

Even among Christians there have been thousands of denominational variations and movements, and every one of them thinks they are right. I grew up in a Baptist church, and we looked forward to the day when we would be in heaven and there would be no more divisions. Some Lutherans would be there, represented by Martin Luther. Methodists would be there, represented by John Wesley. Some Catholics would be there (though this idea was a little more controversial), represented by the pope. And we Baptists would be there, represented by ... Jesus.

Everybody thinks he or she is right — which means that a lot of people are going to find out, when they die, that they were wrong. One of the ironies of atheism is that if there is no such thing as life after death, atheists can never know for sure that they were right, and believers can never know for sure that they were wrong.

I'd like to know. Not just trust, not just hope. I'd like my own bona fide miracle — like my own burning bush or magic fleece or the Cubs winning the World Series in my lifetime.

All this difference of opinion raises a problem. Many people who are smarter than me, better educated than me, and bigger hearted than me cannot even agree with each other. I cannot read every book. Even if I could, I am not smart enough to untangle what perplexes minds far smarter than mine. So how can I choose with any confidence?

During the late nineteenth century, a philosopher-mathematician named William Clifford wrote a hugely influential essay titled "The Ethics of Belief." He argued that it is "always wrong, everywhere, for anyone to believe anything on the grounds of insufficient evidence." Although he didn't say it directly, what he was really writing about was faith in God. He was really saying, "A lot of smart people out there disagree with each other about whether God exists. There is no way to know who is right or who is wrong, so the only appropriate response is, 'Don't decide. Don't commit. Abstain. Opt for doubt.'"

It was around Clifford's era that Thomas Huxley coined the

28

term *agnostic*, which did not exist before the nineteenth century. Agnostics, Huxley said, "totally refuse to commit" to either denying or affirming the supernatural. Huxley himself celebrated René Descartes as the first to train himself to doubt. Descartes' method for knowing was to begin by doubting everything until he found one unshakable belief: *"Cogito ergo sum"* — "I think, therefore I am." (My favorite Cartesian joke: Descartes walks into a bar. "Care for a beer?" asks the bartender. "I think not," says Descartes and disappears.) Huxley said that "doubt had now been removed from the seat of penance ... to which it had long been condemned, and enthroned in that high place among the primary duties."

I get his point. I would like to know for sure. I want to know if it is all true — that God is really there, that Jesus really did drive out demons and walk on water and rise up from the dead on the third day. I would like some assurance that when they play taps over my body down here Someone will be blowing reveille on the other side.

I'd like to *know*. Not just trust, not just hope. I'd like the skies to part sometime. I'd like my own bona fide miracle — like my own burning bush or magic fleece or the Cubs winning the World Series in my lifetime.

And since I can't *know*, Clifford said, I should just settle into the land of "I don't know" and be content with agnosticism.

When Neutrality Is a Bad Choice

But a philosopher named William James responded that sometimes Clifford's advice is bad strategy. He said doubt is the wrong alternative when three conditions are met: when we have live options, when the stakes are momentous, and when we must make a choice.

Sometimes I have to choose between two options even when I cannot prove either one. Cosmic neutrality ignores this problem:

I have to live. I have to make choices. I have to spend my life praying or not praying, worshiping or withholding worship. I have to be guided by some values and desires. And then I have to die. I must give my life in total, in full, without the luxury of holding something back for the second hundred years. My life is the ballot I cast—for God or against him.

My brain cannot provide the certainty that I'm betting my life on the truth. My mortality will not provide the luxury of waiting until I know for sure. There is one road to certainty—through a door marked "death." Then I will know, or there will be no me left to know. But I need to decide how I will live on this side of the door. Once we have been born, trying to put off deciding what to do about God is like jumping off a diving board and trying to put off actually entering the water.

> Our beliefs are not just estimates of probabilities. They are also the instruments that guide our actions.

When I think about this urgency, I'm reminded of a saying my friend Kent the drummer told me about. The background for this saying is that all musicians are torn between the desire for perfection and the demands of reality. They would like to know before they sing a note that it will be pitch-perfect. They would like to know before they hit the drum that the beat will fall in perfect rhythm. But musicians are thwarted by reality. There are no guarantees for the perfection of their choices. In fact, to the contrary, there is the guarantee of imperfection. Kent tells me that no one has ever sung on perfect pitch; no drum has ever been struck in perfect time. So Kent has a saying that reminds him of the need to actually play a note in the face of potential imperfection: "*You have to put it somewhere.* If I refuse to sing a word or play a note until I'm certain of perfection, there will never be music."

If you don't want to go to the grave with all your music in you, you'll have to take a shot. You'll have to roll the dice. You have to accept limits and uncertainty and risks and mistakes. You have to put it somewhere.

Some people choose doubt. But doubt is not always the best strategy. If we followed Clifford's advice, no one would join a political party, take a position on capital punishment, or vote for a school board candidate, because people smarter than us disagree on all these things.

Theologian Lesslie Newbigin writes that we live in an age that favors doubt over faith. We often speak of "blind faith" and "honest doubt." Both faith and doubt can be honest or blind, but we rarely speak of "honest faith" or "blind doubt." Both faith and doubt are needed, yet it is faith that is more fundamental. Even if I doubt something, I must believe there are criteria by which it can be judged. I must believe something before I can doubt anything. Doubt is to belief what darkness is to light, what sickness is to health. It is an absence. Sickness may be the absence of health, but health is more than the absence of sickness. So it is with doubt and faith. Doubt is a good servant but a poor master.

"Doubt is useful for a while.... If Christ spent an anguished night in prayer, if he burst out from the cross, 'My God, my God, why have you forsaken me?' then surely we are permitted doubt. But we must move on. To choose doubt as a philosophy of life is akin to choosing immobility as a means of transportation."

Is Faith or Doubt More Rational?

Doubters often accuse believers of being irrational. But the rationality of belief is a tricky issue. Our beliefs are not just estimates of probabilities. They are also the instruments that guide our actions.

Let's say you manage the Los Angeles Dodgers. It's World Series time — you against the Oakland Athletics. It's the ninth inning, and you're one run behind with one man on base and two outs.

The world's greatest relief pitcher is on the mound. You have two pinch hitters; both of them bat .250. One of them says, "I will probably make an out. There's a three out of four chance I will lose the battle. But at least I will not allow my emotions to cloud my thinking. I will acknowledge the probability of my failure calmly and clearly." The other guy says, "I believe I will get a hit. I have a deep conviction this is my day."

Who do you send to the plate? Would it be more *rational* to send up the logic chopper who thinks he will fail? Wouldn't it make more *sense* to call on Kirk Gibson with his five o'clock shadow and his gimpy knee and his swaggering conviction that he is destined for immortality? You would send the pinch hitter who has all the confidence he could muster. There are *reasons* for faith that go beyond mere evidence. (If you're not a baseball fan, note that Kirk Gibson was a badly injured power-hitting Los Angeles outfielder who in 1988 produced the greatest World Series moment of all time and forever convinced Dodger fans that God not only exists but is in fact a Dodger.)

Let's try another analogy. I'm trapped on the tenth floor of a burning building. The elevator has melted, the stairs have collapsed, and my only escape is to jump out the window into a blanket held by a group of volunteer firemen. The blanket looks thin. Some of the firemen have been celebrating at Octoberfest. Would it be *rational* to say, "I'm not jumping; at best I give them a 10 percent chance of catching me; I may die up here, but I won't jump out the window and risk looking naive"?

Standing in the burning building, I am intensely aware that I am not in the probability calculating game; I am in the survival game. What makes jumping out the window *rational* is that it is the best shot I have at achieving my *purpose*, which is to survive.

The question of faith is never just a question of calculating the odds of God's existence. We are not just probability calculators. We live in a burning building. It's called a body. The clock is ticking.

Let's say we throw in our lot with the doubters. What hopes do I have for a grand purpose in a cul-de-sac? This is how Bertrand Russell, an atheist from a previous century, put it: "In the visible world, the Milky Way is a tiny fragment. Within this fragment the solar system is an infinitesimal speck, and within the speck our planet is a microscopic dot. On this dot, tiny lumps of carbon and water crawl about for a few years until they are dissolved again into the elements of which they are compounded."

Is it only me, or is that just the tiniest bit depressing? Would you want to have that read at your funeral? "There was a little lump of carbon and water crawling around on the speck for a while. Now it's gone. Elvis has left the building. So long."

Maybe old Bertie was right. Maybe the universe is a machine assembled by accident, intended for nothing. Maybe one day it will wind down. Maybe, when the Big Bang collapses in on itself, maybe when the sun expands and the earth is destroyed—maybe then all of life as we know it will end, and it will not have made any difference in that day whether I loved my kids or beat them. We're all just atoms. Maybe so. But I don't know anyone who lives consistently with that idea.

> I do not see how it would be possible to find a meaningful life in a meaningless universe. The only purpose that is worthy of life is something bigger than life itself.

A theologian named Woody Allen captured the absurdity this leaves us in: "More than any time in human history, humankind faces a crossroads. One path leads to despair and utter hopelessness. The other leads to total extinction. Let us pray we have the wisdom to choose correctly."

I do not see how it would be possible to find a meaningful life in a meaningless universe. The only purpose that is worthy of life is something bigger than life itself. It is more than maximizing pleasure and minimizing pain for a few years on earth. The only purpose worthy of life is to be part of a grander vision — the redemption of creation, the pursuit of justice, becoming a saint.

You Are Launched

It is precisely this realization about the human condition that lies behind Blaise Pascal's famous posing of the issue of faith as a wager. Making a decision about faith is more like making a wager than like judging a debate, because in life — as at the roulette table — we have something riding on the outcome.

Some people think Pascal was just making a crude appeal to self-interest. I had two floor-mates in college who worked up what they called the "worst hell" theory of choosing a religion. It worked like this: study all religions, identify the faith that threatens to send people to the worst hell, then join it. Thus you will eliminate at least the worst-case cosmic scenario.

But I don't think that's exactly what Pascal was trying to say. Pascal was a brilliant mathematician. He invented the first calculating machine and the first public transportation system, developed probability theory and much of the mathematics of risk management, and proved the existence of the vacuum — all of which set the stage for quantum physics, the insurance industry, Powerball lotteries and racing forms, vacuum pumps, the atomic bomb, and outer space exploration. He was, as one biographer notes, "the man who invented the modern world."

Pascal was also a wealthy French aristocrat. He was fascinated by gambling, which was an obsession in upper-class seventeenth-century France. His use of the wager was a way of showing that faith is not simply a matter of estimating the probability that God exists. There are certain votes from which it is impossible to abstain, what William James called *forced* decisions. For example, if you decide to put off making a decision about getting in shape, your body will decide for you.

So it is, Pascal said, when it comes to God. Evidence alone cannot clearly indicate that God does or does not exist. However, we must choose whether we will seek him. Not to choose is its own choice. Your wager began the moment you were born. You were "launched." You will bet your life one way or the other. God either exists or he does not. Heads or tails—no third option.

If God does not exist, we lose a life devoted to seeking to love, to live generously, to speak truth, and to do justice. But if God does exist, and we choose not to follow him, we lose everything.

"Everyone believes, for there is no other way to live. Even those who say they *know*, that they have no need of *belief*, are throwing the dice. They are just throwing harder than most." We all have, in the most literal sense, skin in the game.

There is a kind of recent secular version of Pascal's wager. Harvard philosopher Robert Nozick, based on an aspect of modern physics, speculated that it may be impossible for persons to cease to exist. He suggested this approach to life: *first, imagine what form of immortality would be best; then live your life as though it were true.* Nozick died a few years into the new millennium. If it is impossible for persons to cease existing, now he knows.

"Life is a great surprise," Vladimir Nabokov wrote, "I do not see why death should not be an even greater one."

Radical skeptics believe we cannot know anything. There is an old story about a philosophy test on skepticism that consisted of a chair sitting in the middle of a classroom. Students were to solve a single problem: "Prove that this chair exists." One student answered in two words: "What chair?" He got an A.

Skeptics may believe it is impossible to prove that chairs exist. But they still sit down in them.

Radical nihilists believe we *can* know something, and what we know is that there *is* no meaning. We can know that, in Jennifer Hecht's memorable phrase, "the universe is nothing but an accidental pile of stuff, jostling around with no rhyme nor reason, and all life on earth is but a tiny, utterly inconsequential speck of nothing, in a corner of space, existing in the blink of an eye never to be judged, noticed or remembered." But even nihilists, writes Michael Novak, devote beautiful October days to sitting indoors at their computers pecking out messages in the faith that someone will read, that someone will be enlightened, and that what they say will have *meaning* in a universe they claim has none. "They are men and women of faith, our nihilists."

Maybe, as hard as it is to bet on faith, it is even harder to bet on doubt.

Flying and Catching

I think that Clifford was wrong in his essay about the ethics of belief; when it comes to God, it is folly to abstain even when you don't have certainty. I'd put my money on Pascal. But I'm not sure the idea of a wager quite captures the desperate need of the human condition. So I'll try one more picture.

This comes from Henri Nouwen, whose gift to the world was his struggle with pain and faith as the wounded healer. The final year of his life he took a sabbatical from working and writing. He longed for God yet found it hard to pray. He found himself drawn—go figure—to a circus act. A Dutch priest who had taught at Harvard and Yale was hanging out with the greatest show on earth. They were a trapeze act, "The Flying Rodleighs." He watched them perform, and then he got to know them. Trapeze artists usually use a safety net nowadays, but even falling into one of those is dangerous and sometimes fatal.

There were five members in the act—three "flyers" and two "catchers." The flyer climbs the steps, mounts the platform, and grasps the trapeze. He leaps off the platform, swinging through the air. He uses his body for momentum, swinging with increasing speed and height. The catcher hangs from his knees on another trapeze, with his hands free to reach out.

The moment of truth comes when the flyer lets go. He sails into the air with no support, no connection to the earth. He does a somersault or two. Picture him in the middle of a somersault and freeze the frame. There is absolutely nothing, at the moment, to keep the flyer from plunging to his death. What do you think he feels like? Do you think he feels fully alive — every cell in his body screaming out? Think he's feeling any fear right then?

In the next moment the catcher swings into our view. He has been timing his arcs perfectly. He arrives just as the flyer loses momentum and is beginning to descend. His hands clasp the arms of the flyer. The flyer cannot see him; to the flyer everything is a blur. But the flyer feels himself snatched out of the air. The catcher takes the flyer home. And the flyer is very, very glad.

> *The moment of truth comes when the flyer lets go. He sails into the air with no support, no connection to the earth. Do you think he feels fully alive? Think he's feeling any fear right then?*

Nouwen spent some time getting to know the flyers. Flyers are small, weighing 150 pounds or less, because if you're a catcher, you don't want a flyer with a sweet tooth. He learned about the equipment they used. They had socks filled with magnesium dry powder for their hands, especially for Joe, because Joe was one of the catchers. They told Henri, "Joe sweats a lot." If you're a flyer, you don't want a catcher with sweaty hands.

Here's where trusting comes in. Letting go is always an act of trust. Rodleigh, as the leader of the group was called, told Nouwen, "As a flyer, I must have complete trust in my catcher. The public might think I'm the star of the trapeze, but the real star is Joe, my catcher. He has to be there for me with split-second precision and grab me out of the air as I come to him in the long jump."

Nouwen asked him, "How does it work?"

He answered, "The secret is that the flyer does nothing. The catcher does everything. When I fly to Joe, I have simply to stretch out my arms and hands and wait."

Henry asked him, "You do nothing?"

"A flyer must fly and a catcher must catch. The flyer must trust with outstretched arms that his catcher will be there waiting for him."

We are all going to have to let go. But we get to choose to whom we jump. We get to choose—not our level of certainty—but the convictions to which we commit. Believing matters. But there's one other aspect of believing we should know about. Figuring out what we actually believe turns out to be surprisingly difficult. A lot of people think they believe in God, but they really don't.

WHAT KIND OF BELIEF REALLY MATTERS?

Those who believe they believe in God
but without passion in the heart, without anguish of mind,
without uncertainty, without doubt, and even at times without despair,
believe only in the idea of God, and not in God himself.

MADELEINE L'ENGLE

Here's a little experiment: start a sentence with the words "I believe ...," and then finish it with something deeply heartfelt. It is impossible to do without feeling uplifted and stirred.

The need to declare our deeply held beliefs is an irrepressible aspect of being human. In the act of defining what we believe, we define ourselves. I am one who can discern what is true and real and noble and bind myself to it. I believe. One of the most flattering things we can do is ask others their opinion, because what they believe matters.

Sometimes even the notion that human beings are able to form beliefs gets disputed. Daniel Dennett (the philosopher mentioned in chapter 1 as one of the New Atheists) argues that "belief" is not a scientifically valid concept. The analogy he uses involves a chess-playing computer. Computers can't "hold beliefs." Treating one as if it does (as if it believes it must protect its king) can help you *deal* with the computer. But you know that *really* the computer is nothing but circuitry and chips, and circuitry and chips can't *believe* anything. So it is with human beings: we are circuitry and chips. Human beings don't really hold beliefs; it's just useful to treat them as if they do. This is what Daniel Dennett argues.

He doesn't really *believe* it though.

To be is to believe. One important question to ask myself is, what do I *really* believe, and what do I only think I'm *supposed* to believe?

In the Lord of the Rings trilogy, Sam is trying to encourage Frodo not to give up. He reminds Frodo that all the great stories are about characters who keep going when it seems too hard. They all find something to hang on to. "And what about us?" Frodo asks. "What do we have to hang on to?" Sam responds, "That there's good in the world. And it's worth fighting for."

Sometimes our credos are homespun. Sometimes our credos are silly. Sometimes we look for designer beliefs that will show how cool we are.

That one line undid me. I found myself all choked up without even knowing why. I realized later what it was about those words that moved me so: I believed them without trying. Often — partly because of my job — there are statements that I think I *should* believe or that I *want* to believe. Sometimes, because I get paid or applauded for affirming these beliefs, I wonder if I really believe anything at all or if I just talk myself into it because I get rewarded. But my heart said yes with unforced passion to this belief: there is good in the world, and it is worth fighting for.

I believe.

Sometimes our credos are homespun. Robert Fulghum used to

write his out every year. One year he started with "Everything I need to know I learned in kindergarten" and sold a gazillion books.

Sometimes our credos are silly. Countless bumper stickers have been sold bearing the slogan "Everyone has to believe in something. I believe I'll have another beer."

Sometimes we look for designer beliefs that, like designer labels, will show how cool we are. The movie *Bull Durham* was written by a man who grew up in the faith and was disillusioned by the church. It begins with the female lead saying, "I believe in the church of baseball. I've tried all the major religions and most of the minor ones ... and the only church that truly feeds the soul is baseball." Later in the movie the Kevin Costner character recites his creed: "I believe in the soul ... the hanging curve ball, high fiber, good scotch ... I believe there ought to be a constitutional amendment outlawing Astroturf and the designated hitter. I believe in long, slow, deep, soft kisses that last three days." My wife liked that one. A little too much. My wife is a Kevin Costner fundamentalist. Kevin said it; she believes it; that settles it.

What do we *really* believe?

Then there are the great beliefs, beliefs that people have devoted their lives to studying, beliefs that they have argued about and exulted in and sacrificed over and died for:

> *I believe in God, the Father Almighty,*
> *the Creator of heaven and earth,*
> *and in Jesus Christ, his only Son, our Lord:*
> *Who was conceived of the Holy Spirit,*
> *born of the Virgin Mary,*
> *suffered under Pontius Pilate,*
> *was crucified, died, and was buried. . . .*

Sometimes people can rattle off words like that without ever asking themselves if they really believe them. A few years ago a church had just switched to having its liturgies printed by computer. A woman named Edna passed away, and they were able to save time by having the computer print the same order of service they had used for the previous funeral of a woman named Mary; they simply instructed the computer to change each instance of Mary to Edna. It all worked fine until they found themselves reciting from the Apostles' Creed that they believed in Jesus Christ who was conceived by the Holy Spirit and born of the Virgin Edna. ("*That doesn't sound right to me, but I guess if I'm supposed to believe it ...*")

Now, imagine that two people affirm the Apostles' Creed. One person is humble, loving, truthful, surprisingly bold, and full of life, and good-hearted people generally find themselves wanting to be around him. The other man affirms the same beliefs, but he is selfish, angry, judgmental, coldhearted, and proud, and he gossips about people; nobody wants to be around him. Here's the question: Do these two people share the same faith? Do they really believe the same things, and if they do, why are they so different?

But the real question that this is getting at is, If faith is so important, if it is such a big deal to God that we actually say we are saved by grace through faith (Ephesians 2:8) — faith alone — why does faith sometimes not seem to make a bigger difference in people's lives? How can two people have the same faith but be so different? Why doesn't faith make a bigger difference in one's life?

To get at this, let's look at what philosopher Michael Novak speaks of as three different kinds of convictions. We all carry convictions about what we believe, and Novak says we can talk about them in three ways.

Public Convictions

Public convictions are convictions that I want other people to think I believe, even though I really may not believe them. For example,

42

if a certain someone asks me, "Does this dress make my hips look too large?" the correct response is "No. I didn't even know you *had* hips until you mentioned them." I make such statements for "PR" purposes, regardless of whether I really believe them.

Public figures are notorious for stating convictions for the purpose of creating an impression rather than communicating truth ("This is the greatest nation on the face of the earth"; "This is the most momentous election of our lifetimes"). Television comedian Stephen Colbert says the quality to which these statements aspire is *truthiness.* They may not *be* true, but they *sound* true; they allow the speaker to impress people with his or her sincerity.

This has been going on for a long time. After Jesus was born, King Herod said to the wise men, "Go and make a careful search for the child. As soon as you find him, report to me, so that I too may go and worship him" (Matthew 2:8).

> Sometimes being part of a community of faith increases the temptation to pretend to believe what we really don't.

That was not actually Herod's true intent. It was a spin job. We give politicians a hard time for replacing truth with truthiness, but I have an inner politician who puts in overtime, and his main job is crafting and communicating public convictions to help me get what I want.

Sometimes being part of a community of faith increases the temptation to pretend to believe what we really don't. The college I attended required faculty members to sign a document affirming that they believed in premillennialism, a doctrine that Jesus will return to take his followers out of this world before inaugurating a thousand-year earthly reign. Their jobs were contingent on this affirmation. We asked one of our professors why he subscribed to this, since it has been a minority position throughout the history of the church. "My belief in premillennialism hangs by a slender economic thread," he said.

That would be a public conviction. One of the dangers of preaching is that it tempts preachers to pretend they have no doubts and to settle for truthiness.

Private Convictions

Private convictions are convictions that I sincerely *think* I believe, but it turns out they may be fickle. They may be illusory. Although it sounds odd, I may *think* I believe something, but it turns out my true convictions run another way.

For example, I have a friend whom I'll call Maurice Chevalier who had a pattern of fickle private convictions. Maurice would often find himself deeply attracted to some woman when that woman was not available, when she was going out with somebody else. Maurice would sincerely believe that that woman was wonderful, that he would love to be in a romantic relationship with her, that losing her would be tragic. He would tell her that if she would listen. Every once in a while one such woman would break up with her boyfriend and become available. But when she would do that, when she would tell Maurice that she was now free and even eager for the attachment, Maurice would find out that he didn't believe she was so wonderful after all. My wife, who is an incorrigible matchmaker, won't even try to match up Maurice anymore. She now calls this syndrome "Maurice Chevalier disease."

Private convictions seem to be real at the time, but when circumstances shift, they are revealed to be hollow. A biblical example of this took place the night before Jesus died when he predicted that Peter was going to deny him. Peter said: "Even if all fall away, I will not.... Even if I have to die with you, I will never disown you" (Mark 14:29, 31).

When Peter said these words, was he sincere at that moment? Yes, I think he was. Were those convictions true? No. Did Peter feel the same way the next day when the heat was on, when he actually was confronted with the fact that he would have to suffer if he aligned himself with Jesus? No. Sometimes we *think* we have convictions, but it turns out they are fickle. They don't really run deep, and when our circumstances change, we feel differently.

Elmer Gantry was the fictional novel and then movie of a phony early twentieth-century revival preacher. He preached with great force and power on the love of God and the darkness of sin, but in between services he wandered off the sawdust trail to scheme for money, guzzle whiskey, and chase women. A reporter came to know him and was puzzled by the way he could live such a worldly life yet preach with such apparent sincerity and emotion. He asked Gantry if he really believed what he preached. His response: "When I'm preaching, I do." (Elmer Gantry may not be all that well known anymore. Nancy went to a video/music store recently and asked a young clerk if they had *Elmer Gantry*. "I dunno," he said, "what are some of his songs?")

Sometimes private convictions may involve self-deception: we *want* to believe something or are *committed* to believing something even though at some level we know it is false. People with symptoms of a dread disease figure out a way to overlook them; spouses ignore the evidence of a cheating partner; doting parents exaggerate their child's ability.

Friends and I once read a story from the Bible about the prophet Elijah and his servant. They were surrounded by enemies, and the servant was feeling very unsafe. Elijah prayed that God would open his eyes, and suddenly the servant saw that he was surrounded by angels and chariots of fire, that he really was safe in the watchful care of God. Somebody asked, "How would you respond if this were to happen to you?" And one of the people in the group, a really bright man with a PhD who had been in the church his whole life, replied, "I would be surprised to find out what I believed all along turned out to be true."

That sentence has stuck with me. What does it mean to believe something if I'd be surprised if it turned out to be true? "Sometimes it is hard for a tolerably honest man to say what he believes."

Core Convictions

This concept leads to a third level of convictions, and these are the ones that really matter. *Core convictions* are revealed by our daily actions, by what we actually do. They are what might be called the "mental map." Every one of us has one of these mental maps about the way we think things really are and the way life really works.

I believe if I touch fire I will get burned. I believe coffee helps me wake up. I believe in gravity. This is part of my mental map, so I don't have to work hard to behave in a way that is congruent with gravity. I don't have to say, "Today, I'm going to demonstrate my commitment to my belief in gravity." I don't have to remind myself not to jump out of a ten-story building. (On the other hand, if I wanted to hurt myself, I would jump off the building. My actions are always the result of my *purposes* and my *core convictions*.) Gravity is a part of my mental map about the way things really are, and therefore my actions are always congruent with my belief in gravity. This means I will have to become a student of my own behavior to find out what I really believe.

Years ago I took my daughter to a camp in the Upper Peninsula of Michigan. It had no heat, no lights, no electricity at all, no phones, no hot water, no indoor plumbing. It was called Camp Paradise.

I think the name was ironic.

While we were there, we went on a ropes course, and I learned some more about faith. The ropes course stood about thirty feet above the ground, where we had to get from one station to another. Before we went up on the course, we had to sit through a class on safety. We would all be hooked in securely to a safety line. The instructor gave us information about how secure the vests were, about how the carabineers could support thousands of pounds of weight, how the worst that could happen to anyone who slipped is that they would dangle in midair until being rescued.

We all believed the information. If you had given us a test, we all would have affirmed our beliefs in the safety of every step of the ropes course. But a strange thing happened when we got thirty feet off the ground. I found out my body did not believe I was safe. My sweat glands clearly had doubts. My heart rate regulator was nervous. The butterfly squadron in my stomach went into action. I could try to tell my body about the safety information, but it wasn't listening.

However, there were college kids who worked all summer at Camp Paradise. They went up on the ropes course every day. Their bodies believed they were safe. You could see it in the ease of their movements and hear it in their laughter. They did not worry about their fates. Their minds were free to think more interesting thoughts.

What does my body believe?

"Judge not, lest you be judged." I'd like to think I believe this, but my mouth is clearly not convinced.

"Let the one who would be great become a servant." I'd mark this one true on a test, but my hands often have other ideas.

"His eye is on the sparrow." Love the song, but my adrenal system feels the jury is out.

"It is better to give than to receive." I preach messages on this, but the place where my wallet lives is less certain.

> Core convictions are revealed by our daily actions, by what we actually do. They are what might be called the "mental map."

Faith is coming to believe with my whole body what I say I believe with my mind. Another word for this is *paradise*.

So I have three different kinds of convictions. We might think of them in this way: what I *say* I believe; what I *think* I believe; and what I *reveal* I really do believe by my actions.

The best indicator of my true beliefs and my true purposes are my actions. They always flow out of my mental map about the way things really are. What I say I believe might be bogus. What I think I believe might be fickle. But I never violate my idea about the way things are. I always live in a way that reflects my mental map. I live at the mercy of my ideas about the way things really are. Always. And so do you.

Understanding our convictions can help us get at the underlying difference between the two people reciting the Apostles' Creed we talked about earlier in the chapter.

What if the behavior of people who went to church and recited the Apostles' Creed was watched by an all-knowing observer for a year? Then what if these same people were to gather together again and had to recite the "creed" of the beliefs and purposes that really guided their behavior? Do you think that "creed" would look any different from the Apostles' Creed? It would be a little scary, wouldn't it?

True confession: have you been involved in any deception, exaggeration, or distortion over the last year? If your answer is no, you're involved in deception right now. So our true "credo" might involve beliefs like these:

I believe that a lie is a bad thing, but it might be necessary for me to avoid pain. ("A lie is an abomination unto the Lord and a very present help in time of trouble.")

I believe that it pays to be nicest to people who are wealthy, attractive, smart, athletic, successful, or important.

I believe that I have the right to pass judgment on others.

I believe that I have the right to gossip about people.

I believe that I had better be looking out for number one.

I believe that things have not gone as well for me as they should, so I deserve a little treat: another doughnut, another drink, another pill, another fantasy....

I believe that thirty thousand children dying of preventable diseases every day in our world are not worth risking my affluence for.

All of these convictions lie deep within me, and you can see that I believe them if you look at the way I live.

Our behavior also calls into question what we *really* believe about God. For instance, take the belief that God is always present and watching us. If your mom was in the room watching you, you would avoid all kinds of negative behavior. You would not tell what she knew was a lie. You would not read *Playboy* magazine. You just wouldn't. A whole lot of your sinning would be cut down if Mom was always in the room with you. Yet those of us who claim to believe God is always present and watching do these and/or darker things all the time. Do we *really* believe he's watching? Are we able to push such beliefs aside when we want to?

When someone claims to believe one way yet acts another, we call this *bad faith*. *Good faith*, on the other hand, is congruence between what we claim to believe and how we actually live. If someone intends to buy a house, the down payment is a gesture of good faith. Good faith means not deceiving others (in our public convictions) and not deceiving ourselves (in our private convictions.) Good faith means loving the truth more than we love ourselves.

> When someone claims to believe one way yet acts another, we call this bad faith. Good faith is congruence between what we claim to believe and how we actually live.

49

Jesus' Convictions

The testimony of those who claimed to know Jesus was that there was a remarkable congruence about him. What he said and what he thought were in harmony with what he did. He was the Man of good faith.

He was also a teacher. What kind of convictions do you think Jesus is most interested in changing — public, private, or core convictions?

Like any good teacher, he is most interested in people's core convictions about the way things truly are. This is faith at the level where it really matters.

However, merely knowing about the different levels of conviction does not change much. I can understand the distinctions, but I cannot even imagine what it would be to have the mental map of Jesus. We are coming to the deep end of the pool here, and I am just a wader, so all I can do is point.

Here's how it worked for the disciples. Jesus appeared, and he lived with a new kind of mental map that was in perfect agreement with the reality of God and God's kingdom and God's presence breaking through right here. Congruence existed between what Jesus *said* and what Jesus *thought* and what Jesus *did*. He believed that there was a heavenly Father who was always present with him, always loved him. Jesus believed that in the way that I believe in the reality of gravity.

The disciples looked at Jesus, and they thought, *I like his life. I wish I could live like that.* When they tried doing the things that Jesus instructed, they found that his teachings actually made sense when they acted on them. Forgiving worked better than vengeance. Generosity worked better than hoarding. They began to believe these truths for themselves.

The growth of the disciples looked something like this: *First they had faith* in *Jesus; then they began to have the faith* of *Jesus.* Their mental maps began to look like Jesus' mental map. Finally, after his crucifixion and resurrection and the coming of the Holy Spirit, his disciples realized that Jesus is the Savior of the world—that he really is the revelation of God himself—and therefore they trusted him with their eternal destinies as well. Elton Trueblood wrote these words, and I think they are profoundly true: "The deepest conviction of the Christian is that Christ was not wrong."

Faith involves certain beliefs. Faith involves an attitude of hope and confidence. But at its core, faith is trusting a person.

Nevertheless, we often try to get people to trust Jesus for eternity —to get them into heaven—without their first learning to trust him for their daily lives. As a matter of psychological reality, this just does not work. It produces people who *say* they trust Jesus and who might even *think* they trust Jesus, but what they *do* shows that they do not share his ideas about the way things really are and the way life really works. Therefore they are not able to live the way that Jesus would live in their place. It is hard to live as Jesus would live if we do not share at the core level his convictions about the way things really are. This is why James wrote, "What good is it, my brothers and sisters, if people claim to have faith but have no deeds? Can such faith save them?... Show me your faith without deeds, and I will show you my faith by what I do" (James 2:14, 18 TNIV).

> *Faith involves certain beliefs. Faith involves an attitude of hope and confidence. But at its core, faith is trusting a person.*

Some people who claim to be Christians are selfish, greedy, and judgmental. Don't ask me how I know. Others are humble and generous. Both may *say* they trust Jesus. Both may *think* they trust Jesus. But their mental maps—their convictions about the way things really are—are night and day away from each other and produce two different kinds of people and two different kinds of souls even though they affirm the same creed. I think this is why I have sometimes found myself more drawn to someone who is "outside the faith" than to another person who is considered a leader of it.

Let's say one person has a public creed that is 100 percent orthodox and private convictions that are 100 percent orthodox, but his mental map leads to greed, selfishness, arrogance, and lovelessness. And he's moving in the wrong direction.

Another person does not look very orthodox in his theology; internally he is filled with doubts and uncertainty. But his mental map, on issues of generosity, forgiveness, grace, and love, is ten times closer to Jesus' mental map than the first person's. And he's moving in the right direction.

Which person has more faith? Which one is a "believer"?

Frederick Buechner put it like this: "Thus many an atheist is a believer without knowing it, just as many a believer is an atheist without knowing it. You can sincerely believe there is no God and live as though there is. You can sincerely believe there is a God and live as though there isn't. So it goes."

Interestingly, Jesus never said, "Believe my arguments." He said, "Follow me." Jesus himself had his own kind of "Pascalian wager" at this point. At the end of his longest recorded talk, he told a story about the construction business, in which houses get built wisely or foolishly. It always reminds me of the story of the three little pigs. Each character builds a house. Each house faces a test. Houses built wisely survive; houses built foolishly crumble.

Here is the challenge of the story: We all are house builders. Our houses are our lives, and we construct them out of the choices we make day by day. Like it or not. This is not optional. We are launched. We have to put our houses somewhere.

We all are storm facers. We all will face trials and ultimately death. The big bad wolf is coming our way. This is not optional.

We will choose how we construct our lives. We will choose the convictions we build them on. We can build them on rock or straw. We can make them of wood, hay, or brick.

The risk doesn't go away. We cannot know ahead of time how the house will stand up to the storm. Still, we all have to build a house. But will we ever get home?

LONGING FOR HOME

I have become aware,
not by my own wish, almost against my will,
of an existence of another life of far, far greater importance
and beauty than this physical one.

HUGH WALPOLE

George Carlin used to do a routine about the difference between football and baseball:

> Football is played on a gridiron. Baseball is played in a park.
>
> Football players wear helmets. Baseball players wear caps.
>
> In football the specialist comes in to kick something. In baseball the specialist comes in to relieve somebody.
>
> Baseball has the seventh-inning stretch. Football has the two-minute warning. Baseball gets extra innings. Football has sudden death.
>
> In football the runner gives you the stiff arm. In baseball the runner gets to slide. *Wheee.*
>
> But the biggest difference is that in football the main object is military. The battle is fought in the trenches, the field

general (quarterback) seeks to evade the blitz and soften up the enemy line with a pounding ground attack and aerial bombardment. Sometimes he uses bullet passes; when he thinks it will work, he goes for a bomb to riddle the enemy defenses and penetrate the end zone.

In baseball, the object is to go home.

That one spot on the baseball field is different from all the other places. It's the place where you start the game. You can't stay there. You have to leave to try to get to first base, then second base, then third. You'd think the next one would be called fourth base. But it's not. It's called "home." When you leave it, you're vulnerable. But if you make it back, no one can get you out.

You're safe at home.

Author Joe Kraus notes that home, in both baseball and in life, is surprisingly hard to define. In real life what makes a place "home"? Home is the place where you're safe. Home is the place where your story begins. Other people can't bother you there. When you're home, you're free. You can walk around in your underwear, let the dog kiss you on the lips, and have Coke for breakfast, and nobody gets to criticize you. (Joe Kraus doesn't live where I live, that's for sure.)

When you're home, you're protected. Even the police can't enter your home unless they receive permission.

You may hang up your clothes in a *house*. But *home* is where you belong. Home is part of what makes you you.

> It takes a heap o' livin' in a house t' make it home,
> A heap o' sun an' shadder, an' ye sometimes have t' roam
> Afore ye really 'preciate the things ye lef' behind,
> An' hunger fer 'em somehow, with 'em allus on yer mind.

Longing for Home

To not be home is to invite a strange disease we call homesickness: feelings of longing and desire, often mixed with anxiety and depression, caused by separation from the place we belong. You can be staying at the Ritz-Carlton but still miss your little shack if the shack is home.

If there is a God, we have hope for home. If there is not a God, we are the homeless race.

Biologist Stuart Kauffman wrote a book titled *At Home in the Universe*, in which he notes that people once understood themselves to be the chosen of God, made in his image, keeping his word in a creation wrought by his love for us. "Now ... we find ourselves on a tiny planet, on the edge of a humdrum galaxy among billions like it.... We are but accidents, we're told. The universe now appears utterly indifferent. We bustle but are no longer at home."

When you're home, you belong. Home is the place where you are valued. You and your home bless each other. If you didn't have a home, you would be homeless; you wouldn't belong anywhere.

On the other hand, if your home didn't have you, it would be just another place.

Robert Frost wrote a poem in which a husband and a wife argue about whether to take in an old and troublesome acquaintance who is dying and has nowhere else to go. The wife thinks they should invite him in; the husband recognizes that he will probably have to agree but feels trapped. It leads them to reflect on what a home really is. The husband says, "Home is that place where, when you go there, they have to take you in." But his wife disagrees. "I would say, rather, home is what you don't have to deserve." Is it obligation that makes a home, or is it grace?

A friend of mine named John works with street hustlers, desperate young men in their late teens who turn tricks in gay neighborhoods of Chicago. He brought one seventeen-year-old boy into his home to have Thanksgiving dinner with his family.

> To be homeless means more than looking for a place to sleep at night. It is an attack on our identity, on the possibility of knowing who we are.

"I've never done this before," the boy whispered shyly to John.

"Never done what?" John asked.

"I've never done the dinner thing; sitting around a table eating a meal with a family. I've never done this...."

To be homeless means more than looking for a place to sleep at night. It is devastating to the soul. It means not belonging. It is an attack on our identity, on the possibility of knowing who we are.

At Home in the Universe

Are human beings at home in the universe? Are we here by invitation or by accident? Are we family or strange carbon-based intruders? Are we homesick because we have no home or because we are away from home?

Some people believe that all we can ever know about our world is what we learn through science, and that if we trust in science, we will have to give up our faith. Much that is written about the conflict between faith and science in our day is based on misunderstanding. For instance, sometimes people think that if you take Genesis seriously, you cannot believe in the Big Bang or a process of natural selection. Journalist A. J. Jacobs writes of his struggle to believe in God if it means believing — with literal six-day creationists — that the world is barely older than Gene Hackman. But this is to misunderstand Genesis, which was not written with a twenty-first-century science agenda in mind. To take one example, in the Genesis account, the sun doesn't make its appearance until the fourth day. Even in ancient times, people were pretty much aware that the sun played a crucial part in daylight. The purpose of the writer was not to talk about when the sun showed up. When Genesis was written, the sun was widely worshiped. And the writer wanted to make sure people knew not to worship the sun, that the sun was created like everything else. Ancient people generally understood this about the Bible.

Over fifteen hundred years ago, Augustine wrote a fascinating book called *The Literal Meaning of Genesis*. In this book he says:

Often a non-Christian knows something of the earth, the heavens, the motions and the orbits of the stars, and this knowledge he holds with certainty from reason and experience. It is thus offensive and disgraceful for an unbeliever to hear a Christian talk nonsense about such things, claiming that what he is saying is based on Scripture. We should do all we can to avoid such embarrassment, which people see as ignorance in the Christian and laugh to scorn.

The writer of Genesis was not writing a modern-day science book. He wanted to say that the universe is good and that it was made to be our home; that we have fallen and home is messed up; that it will take God to set it right again.

Deeper questions are at play. Oxford theologian Richard Swinbourne writes, "It is extraordinary that there should exist anything at all. Surely the most natural state of affairs is simply nothing: no universe, no God, nothing. But there is something." Notions like the "Big Bang" and natural selection and evolution explain how the mechanism of change might take place, but they do not explain how existence springs from nothing. The old man in Marilynne Robinson's wonderful novel *Gilead* muses, "Existence seems to me now the most remarkable thing that could ever be imagined."

The real trick isn't changing one thing into another thing. The real trick is creating something out of absolutely nothing.

A group of scientists decided that human beings had come a long way and no longer needed God. They picked one scientist to go and tell God that they did not need him anymore. The scientist went to him and said, "God, we can make it on our own. We know how life started. We know the secret. We know how to clone it. We know how to duplicate it. We can do it without you."

God listened patiently and said, "All right. What do you say we have a man-making contest?"

The scientist said, "Okay, great. We'll do it."

God said, "Now we're going to do it just the way I did back in the old days with Adam."

The scientist said, "Sure, no problem." He reached down and grabbed a handful of dirt, and God said, "No, no, no. You go get your own dirt."

That's the trick.

Talking about something that changes into something else and how long it takes for something to change into something else — that's not what most cries out for explanation. The trick is how do you get from nothing to something, and why is there something? We all want to know.

> *The trick is how do you get from nothing to something, and why is there something? We all want to know.*

Cosmic Homelessness

If there is no God, there is no home. The universe is a blind and pitiless machine. Human beings appeared in it by accident. We have minds and consciousness and desires and hopes, but the forces of the universe will one day crush them all, and us along with them. We don't belong here. The Bible, on the other hand, indicates that the reason we love the earth so much is that God made it to be our home.

The first home was called the garden of Eden. The story of the fall is, among other things, a reflection of our homesickness.

God told human beings to exercise dominion over the earth. That means it is our home but that it is really a gift. The deed is in his name. We are supposed to take care of it. Richard Foster writes, "We plant evergreens and compost garbage, we clean a room and put coasters under glasses, and in these ways we help to tidy up Eden."

Because our homes are so wrapped up with our identities, we become deeply attached to them. Most of our kids' childhood they lived on Eisenhower Circle in a suburb of Chicago, in a two-story white house with red shutters and a patio on a pie-wedge lot with a big backyard. We raised them there and watched them trudge off to school, have sleepovers in the basement, go on first dates, practice piano, and mess up the kitchen learning how to cook.

When we sold the place, our furniture got moved across country a week before we did, so we stayed with friends during our final week in Illinois. Our answering machine was still in the house, so Nancy asked me to pick it up one night after work.

I was unprepared for the emotion that hit me when I walked through that empty house. I thought of how our children had grown up there, and how when I was gone and they were old, they would still think of this house as the home of their childhood. I walked around talking to each room. "You were a good old house," I told it. "You were good to my children. I'm so glad you were my home. There will be other houses for me, I know, but none of them will mean to me what you did."

How was I to know there was a real estate agent in the back bedroom?

War of the Worlds

We have learned unspeakable volumes about the physical nature of our universe, but we have lost confidence that it was intended to be our home. "Once upon a time the universe had meaning." So begins a superb book called *Medieval Views of the Cosmos*. Our problem since then is not that science has taught us much. It's not that science has taught us our world has no meaning. Our problem is that we have decided that what cannot be answered by science cannot be answered at all. Science can tell us how a house gets built, but it cannot tell us what makes a house a home.

We now have two separate worlds: the inner world of *persons*: thoughts and hopes and griefs and convictions within us, and the external world of *objects*: quarks and germs and galaxies outside us. They seem to be at odds with one another. And ironically it is the world of persons — the only reality we have direct access to — that we are no longer sure of.

Homes mean protection to us, yet bad things happen even in our homes. Sigmund Freud wrote about our experience of what he called the uncanny — that which is both familiar and yet terrifying. The uncanny frightens us because it almost — but not quite — brings to mind what we have repressed. The haunted house is one of the most vivid species of the uncanny. The German word for uncanny is *unheimlich* — literally "unhomelike."

The world was made to be our home, yet it is not our home. It has gone wrong. But perhaps this sense of "not being at home" in my world tells me something about me.

Homesickness as Clue to Our Condition

I am not home.

We run away from home. I was mistreated once — I don't remember how, but I'm sure it was bad — and I told my parents I was leaving. I packed my very small suitcase and told my mother to call my grandfather; then I sat outside on the curb waiting for him to pick me up.

An hour later, my mom came outside. "He's not coming, you know," she said.

"Why not?" I asked.

"Well, for one thing, because he's already raised his family. For another thing, you're not his son. You're our son. And for another thing, you're seventeen years old. You're too old to run away."

But you're never too old to run away from home. Jesus' most famous story is about a son who runs away from home. First the son doubts that he wants to be home. Then he doubts that home will take him back.

"Home is that place where, when you go there, they have to take you in."

"I would say, rather, home is what you don't have to deserve."

Jesus was saying that the story of the human race is the story of a runaway. And of a father who keeps waiting for his child to come home.

> Our problem is not that science has taught us our world has no meaning. Our problem is that we have decided that what cannot be answered by science cannot be answered at all.

Ever wonder where God calls home? The Greeks wrote of anthropomorphic gods living and fighting and loving at Olympus. And the Norse gods used to have drinking parties in the halls of Valhalla.

The Roman philosopher Lucretius thought such ideas were undignified, that the true gods were serene beings living in "quiet habitations, never shaken by storms. . . . All their wants are supplied by nature, and nothing at any time cankers their peace of mind." They are "ideals of contentment and serenity who by definition cannot be bothered with human beings and their petty problems." We are, Lucretius thought, to emulate them. But we cannot contact them, we cannot visit their home, for they cannot be troubled. Lucretius was considered an atheist in his day because, although he did not deny the existence of a god, he denied the possibility of contact with one.

Jesus had a different idea. "If anyone loves me," he said, "he will obey my teaching. My Father will love him, and we will come to him and make our home with him" (John 14:23).

I have a friend named Max who is in his eighties and has been married to his wife, Esther, for sixty years. They could live anywhere, but they live in Michigan. I asked him why. He said Esther likes Michigan. I asked him, "But what about you, Max?"

He said, "I decided a long time ago that home is where Esther is."

Home for Max is less about a place than a person.

Maybe there is no God. Then the universe is not a home, just an accident. Maybe there is a God, but he lives in quiet habitations, untroubled by petty human problems. Or maybe God can make himself so small and vulnerable as to take up residence in a human heart—and break when it is broken. Maybe home is where God is. And maybe it will be awhile before we feel at home.

Ask anyone who has lived in the same home a long time if there is anything wrong with it. We all have a list of home repairs we intend to get around to. At first they bother us intensely. After a while, what changes isn't that we fix them; we just get used to them.

In our home on Eisenhower Circle, we had a dog named Chestnut that used to eat the furniture. I don't mean he gnawed on it. I don't mean he got teeth marks on it. When I say he ate the furniture, I mean he ate the furniture. We had a sofa with an ottoman whose entire cover had been eaten off, along with about half the Styrofoam stuffing.

I didn't even notice.

Every once in a while we'd have a guest over and my wife would glare at me with one of those "How many times have I asked you to do something about this?" looks. Our home needed rehabilitation, needed to be changed so it would be fit for habitation.

So it is with my heart. I don't even notice, but my Guest does. We are not home.

Coming Home...

Bible teacher Ray Vander Laan notes that we can learn much about Jesus' teachings when we understand home life in the ancient Near East. Many people lived in what was called an *insula*, a ranch-style floor plan arranged around a common courtyard. A home like that tended to house multiple generations at once if you were fortunate enough to live that long.

When a son got engaged, the new couple did not generally go house hunting. The paternal family would just add another room to the insula, and then the new couple would move in.

Often in Jesus' wedding stories he would talk about announcements going out to people that the time for the wedding had come. This is because dates got arranged a little differently in those days. Nowadays couples pick a wedding date far in advance on the calendar. Back then a couple would get betrothed, but even they wouldn't know the actual wedding date. They would have to wait while the building program got under way. The father would simply add another room to the house. When the father said the room was ready, he would tell his son, and the son would announce to his bride that the room was ready. Then the announcements would go out.

The writers of Scripture sometimes used the image of home life to describe our place in the universe. One of the most poignant uses involves the idea that the church—people like you and me—is the bride and Jesus is the groom.

We long for home because we know we are not fully there yet. Thus the Bible says we should not let our souls get too wrapped up around what it calls "the world." The writer of Hebrews says that the heroes of the faith knew this. They did not regard any place as home. They considered themselves as strangers and aliens (11:13). But this was not because they thought of themselves as homeless. Home was somewhere else.

"Do not let your hearts be troubled," Jesus said. "Trust in God; trust also in me. In my Father's house are many rooms; if it were not so, I would have told you. I am going there to prepare a place for you" (John 14:1–2).

Every once in a while we get a glimpse of what home could be like. Those are the moments when faith gets born.

THE LEAP

Faith is a footbridge
that you don't know will hold you up over the chasm
until you're forced to walk out onto it.

NICHOLAS WOLTERSTORFF

Mountains have always been God-places. A mountain, if you think about it, is where heaven and earth come closest to each other. And there is something transcendent about a mountain. A mountain is a place of vision. In ancient times the remoteness and inaccessibility of mountains gave them an aura of mystery and power. Still today they produce a sense of wonder and awe that there is a higher reality. We are mountain climbers. We are mountain seekers.

Height is always suggestive to us of transcendence and power and vision. We venerate height. In the ancient world, altars were generally built on "high places," where sacrifices would be offered by high priests. Even today we speak of high ideals and high achievements, and politicians run for high office. People of greater height actually make higher salaries than shorter people. When someone becomes pretentious, we tell him to get off his high horse. We use drugs to give us a sense of temporary transcendence, give them names like "ecstasy," and say they make us "high." When we become addicted, we seek the help of a higher power.

Great heights inspire us, but they also humble us. They speak to us of our own smallness. No matter how hard we try, human beings are unable to refrain from worship. "The one essential condition of human existence is that man should always be able to bow down before something infinitely great."

When a subject comes before a king, he kneels down. He is acknowledging that he is in the presence of his master. When a believer—in any religion—prays to his god, he kneels down. He is acknowledging that he is in the presence of his master. When a young man asks a woman to marry him, he gets down on one knee. He is acknowledging that he is in the presence of his master.

One of God's most important names, used some fifty times in the Bible is "Most High." All the signals of transcendence point toward him. He is over all. In him we come to the mountain that cannot be conquered or measured.

Sometimes we make it to the mountaintop. It is on the mountaintop where we see.

Where Faith Is Born

A mountaintop experience is that moment when you suddenly find yourself able to believe. You are able to see. You hear an inspirational talk. You watch the birth of a child. You receive an answer to prayer. Sometimes it's beauty that pierces your heart—a series of notes in a song, a phrase in a book—and you know that God is there. Faith is born.

Philosopher Alvin Plantinga says that we have a kind of special faculty, a *sensus divinitatis*, that is triggered by "the marvelous, impressive beauty of the night sky; the timeless crash and roar of the surf that resonates deep within us; the majestic grandeur of the mountains," even "awareness of guilt." Just as bats have radar and dogs can hear dog whistles, we have moments when it is clear to us that "things are not what they seem." "I have seen things," Aquinas told a friend, "that make all my writings seem like straw."

Those moments may be as simple as seeing a flower and finding ourselves believing that it was designed by God. Or they may be mysterious. They may be beyond our power to explain or describe. They may be the kind of high people use drugs as a shortcut to. There are stories of mystics who pray for hours as if for minutes; see visions, dream dreams.

> *A mountaintop experience is that moment when you suddenly find yourself able to believe. You know that God is there. Faith is born.*

When French philosopher and mathematician Blaise Pascal died, a piece of paper was found sewn in his cloak. He had written it nine years earlier, on Monday, November 23, 1654. Before then he had been wildly successful and deeply unhappy. On that Monday night, he met God.

People knew that Pascal had changed. One day he had been drowning in confusion; the next he was free of it. One day he had been unhappy with his life, disgusted with his world and himself, and then there was a change in his soul. My own favorite indicator was that he began to make his own bed. He began to rely less and less on his servants. He became one of the servants.

But Pascal never told anyone about his "night of fire," never breathed a word. No one would have known, except after Pascal died, his nephew and a servant were sorting through Pascal's clothing when the servant found what he thought was extra padding. It turned out to be a piece of crumpled parchment with a faded piece of paper. Pascal had sewn it into his clothes so he could wear it next to his heart. These were the words he had penned:

Fire.
GOD of Abraham, GOD of Isaac, GOD of Jacob.
Not the God of the philosophers and of the learned.
Certitude. Certitude. Feeling. Joy. Peace.
GOD of Jesus Christ ...
Forgetfulness of the world and of everything, except GOD.
Grandeur of the human soul.
Joy, Joy, Joy, tears of joy ...

Often our mountaintop moments are connected with our lowest valleys. One day when we were sophomores in college, my friend Chuck woke up and simply knew that God did not exist. There was no apparent reason why this happened. He wasn't troubled by doubt. He was troubled by certainty. It was suddenly just clear to him that God did not exist. Chuck had been a Christian for many years; he prayed, read the Bible, went to a Christian school, and dated a Christian girl. But one night he knew there was no God just like you know there is no Easter Bunny. A few of us went to his room to talk to him; it was as if someone had died. Because for him, in those hours, someone had died.

He prayed a desperation prayer: "God, if you're there, I need you to do something. I need to get a call from my mother." And although this sounds like a scene from a movie, a few moments later, out of the blue, his mother called. And Chuck could believe again. Not without doubt, but with hope.

My first adviser in graduate school was a psychologist named Lee Edward Travis. Dr. Travis was a legend; he wrote the definitive textbook on speech pathology, introduced electroencephalograph research to the United States, and was ranked among the thirteen most influential psychologists in the country in the mid-twentieth century. When he was almost sixty-five years old, he walked into a church for the first time in forty years. While sitting in the pew, he had a full-blown experience of the presence of God. Visions, voices, assurances of God's presence and care — stuff he would have medicated anybody else for. This seriously messed with his professional life. The upper echelons of the American Psychological Association were not a hotbed of evangelicalism. He spent the next twenty-five years founding and leading the first Christian doctoral program in clinical psychology to be accredited by the APA. He never had another encounter like his first one.

My great-grandfather, Robert Bennett Hall, lost his mom and dad when he was an infant and grew up in an orphanage. He hated the orphanage and ran away when he was barely in his teens. He was taken in by a storekeeper who allowed him to live with him in exchange for working at the store. He married the storekeeper's daughter and was sweeping the store out one day when he received "the call." He put down the broom, folded up the apron, and spent the next sixty years preaching in little churches across Illinois and Indiana. My cousin has my great grandfather's old record book: he often got paid for preaching with eggs or hens or, every once in a while, five dollars.

We are drawn to the mountain. It is suggestive that there never has been a society that began with an atheistic or naturalistic culture. Always human beings have begun with a story. Always they have begun with faith. Doubt always comes later.

Leaving the Mountain

But doubt always comes. Here's the sad truth about the mountaintop: no one is allowed to remain there permanently. Everyone has to return to the valley of ambiguity.

This means that we can expect that our sense of certainty about our beliefs will ebb and flow. Sometimes doubt will come. But — and this is the important part — doubts do not always come because we have been given new evidence against our faith. One of the biggest illusions we have about our minds is that they are generally governed by reason. But our minds are not logic machines.

What seems true to us in one moment can change drastically in the next.

Several years ago, when I lived in Southern California, I had a friend who liked to hang glide. He took me up on a mountain to watch him. He said he was going to give me a gift up on the mountain. We went up there, and it was beautiful. When you're on a mountain, the sight is scenic and inspiring.

Other people would hang glide off that same mountain. It was a popular spot. After we arrived, some people came over and gave us a little lecture about safety and showed us the equipment. They showed us how strong the harnesses were and explained the aero-dynamics of hang gliding. They talked about how the odds of death related to hang gliding are only about one in one thousand. They gave us this lecture while we were sitting in a parking lot — in safety. I believed what they said. It all made sense. And then my friend said, "Okay, now here's the gift that I'm giving you today. Today you are going to hang glide with me. Today you are going to jump off this mountain."

> One of the biggest illusions is that our minds are generally governed by reason. But our minds are not logic machines. What seems true to us in one moment can change drastically in the next.

I walked over to the edge of the cliff and stood there. What do you think happened to my sense of certainty as I moved from safety over to the edge of the cliff? Do you think my sense of certainty and safety went up or down? It went way down. My mind was suddenly flooded with doubts. What if the harness unbuckled? What if the wings failed? What if there was a rogue tornado? What if I was attacked by a large bird? I saw my body splattered down there on the ground. I imagined my children without a father. I saw Nancy without a husband ... dating other men ... wealthy and attractive men of whom I did not approve.

Objectively, nothing had changed from the parking lot to the edge of the cliff. I had received no new evidence that would incline me intellectually to think that hang gliding was less safe. I had no new information, yet my mind was suddenly flooded with doubt. That is what often happens when I move from safety to the edge.

I had a choice to make. You don't "partly" step off a mountain. Either you jump or you stay put. This is sometimes called "the leap of faith." If you want to fly, if you ever want to soar, you have to take that leap. Your mind may have all kinds of fears and doubts running through it, but if you want to fly, you have to take the leap. And I did. It was fabulous. I've never done it again, but it was pretty cool.

The idea of a leap of faith (a term often associated with Danish philosopher Søren Kierkegaard, who was not just a brilliant mind but also a Scandinavian) has frequently been misunderstood. It does not mean choosing to believe an impossible thing for no good reason. Sometimes people talk about it as if it is the "leap" in which you ignore evidence, give up on reason, and embrace fantasy. But *leap* was Kierkegaard's term for a genuinely free action. Any freely chosen commitment is a leap, such as the choice to marry or to bear children. The move from innocence to sin is also a leap.

The leap of faith is a "leap" because it involves making a total commitment. It can be made for good reasons — reasons we have carefully considered. But it is nevertheless a leap, because we have to commit in spite of our fears and doubts, for there is no other way to soar, no other way to fly.

Certain fundamental decisions in life require 100 percent commitment — passionate engagement. Kierkegaard spoke of faith as a "passion." Certain decisions require intense commitment — for example, to live by certain values, to get married, to raise a child (there are no guarantees that the child won't break your heart), to have a friend, to follow God. And some decisions, generally the most important ones, require total commitment but do not give any guarantees.

Mortimer Adler was one of the great philosophers of the twentieth century. He was for many decades convinced by philosophical arguments — for instance, the argument from design — that there must be a God. He believed such arguments show that there must be a powerful, intelligent, personal force behind creation.

> *If I leap, if I trust,*
> *I do not know for sure*
> *what will happen.*
> *What I do know is this:*
> *if I don't leap,*
> *if I don't trust,*
> *if I don't hope,*
> *if I don't ask,*
> *I will never soar.*

But he did not worship this being, for he believed that these philosophical arguments could not show that such a being was *good* and was interested in him. He believed in a god as he believed in the ozone layer.

Then one day as an old man he lay sick in a hospital bed. A friend came to pray for him, and while his friend was praying, Mortimer Adler found tears streaming down his face and found himself praying. He knew only one prayer — the Lord's Prayer. He found himself praying it day after day — and *believing*.

He said the leap of faith was, for him, not a "jump to conclusions" based on insufficient evidence. It was a leap from assent to devotion. "The god of philosophers is not a god to be loved, worshiped, or prayed to. A god who is not concerned with human destiny by being law-giving and grace-giving is the god of philosophical and irreligious deists," not the self-revealing God of the Bible.

If I leap, if I trust, I do not know for sure what will happen.

What I do know is this: if I don't leap, if I don't trust, if I don't hope, if I don't ask, I will never soar. I will never know. I will live and grow old and die standing on the side of that cliff.

Life Down Below the Mountain

In Ezekiel 28 the prophet says that the garden of Eden was set on a mountain. The fall meant leaving Eden, which meant leaving the mountain. But God would still give people mountaintop moments. God met Abraham on Mount Moriah. God spoke to Moses in a burning bush on Mount Horeb. "When Moses came down from Mount Sinai ..., he was not aware that his face was radiant because he had spoken with the LORD. When Aaron and all the Israelites saw Moses, his face was radiant, and they were afraid to come near him" (Exodus 34:29–30). God spoke to Elijah in a "still small voice" on a mountain. But after meeting God there, people would always have to leave the mountain and face life down below.

Jesus would often go to the mountaintop to pray, to be with his Father. So Peter, James, and John were not really surprised when Jesus took them with him one day up to a mountain. The mountain is sometimes called the Mount of Transfiguration, and it is a hinge point in the New Testament story of Jesus. In Mark's account he deliberately echoes what happened on Mount Sinai: this time it is Jesus who becomes radiant.

Peter gets to see Jesus transformed on the mountaintop. He responds by suggesting they stay on the mountain and in a comment of staggering incomprehension, suggests that they build shelters for Jesus and Elijah and Moses, because "he did not know what to say" (9:6).

Of course, when you don't know what to say, one option is to say nothing, but this apparently did not occur to Peter. And even though he had this mountaintop experience, it did not prevent him from denying Jesus outright when the pressure was on.

Why can't we always stay on the mountain? A nine-year-old girl name Rosy asked me, "If God loves us so much, why doesn't he make us happy all the time?"

I don't know. Maybe it is because, as important as happiness is, there are other things that must happen, like becoming good, so that happiness doesn't become the wrong kind of "god." Maybe if I spend too much time on the mountain, I will be in danger of worshiping the mountain where I met God instead of worshiping God. I'll just want the experience, the feeling, the high.

Philip Yancey notes that there is something unpredictable about faith. Nine times in the Gospels Jesus says to people, "Your faith has healed you." But he often praises faith in unlikely people. In fact, often it is foreigners who show the greatest faith. A Roman centurion tells Jesus that Jesus does not even need to come to his home to perform a healing; he believes that all Jesus has to do is speak a word and it will be so. Jesus is amazed: "I have not found anyone in Israel with such great faith," he says (Matthew 8:10). A Canaanite woman pesters Jesus to help her daughter when Jesus is on retreat. He seems to put her off, reminding her that he was sent to the lost sheep of Israel and not the Gentile "dogs." But she persists in this strange tug-of-war until Jesus gives in or perhaps allows to be revealed in her what he knew was there all along, exclaiming, "Woman, you have great faith!" (Matthew 15:28). Why does faith so often thrive where it is least expected? Why do suffering and persecution — intended to destroy faith — so often strengthen it instead?

> If I spend too much time on the mountain, I may be in danger of worshiping the mountain where I met God instead of worshiping God. I'll just want the experience, the feeling, the high.

"Christianity is like a nail," Yemelian Yaroslavsky, chairman of Stalin's League of the Militant Godless, complained. "The harder you strike it, the deeper it goes.

What I do know is that Jesus always says the same thing: "Time to leave the mountain now. Time to go down below."

The Valley of "If"

Jesus said to Peter, James, and John, "The Son of Man must suffer much and be rejected" (Mark 9:12), and (in so many words) "You'll have to walk through it with me. You'll have to go through confusion and doubt; you'll have to ask questions and struggle. There will be a crucifixion. Then there will be a resurrection, and on the other side, the day is coming when you are going to soar, but not yet. Not today. Today you have to trust me. We're going to have to go down off the mountain."

They go down below, and things are not going as well down there. They meet a father who is desperate for help. His son is tormented by a demon and suffers convulsions and self-destructive behavior. He is looking for Jesus, and some of the disciples tell him that Jesus is up on the mountain. He asks, "Can you help me? This is killing my son." The disciples say, "Okay." They have watched Jesus pray. They have watched him heal and deliver. They say the same things that Jesus has said, but this time the words don't take ... don't stick ... don't work.

A crowd of people are watching. Some of them are religious leaders who don't believe in Jesus and don't follow him. They watch the disciples fail and say things like, "Apparently this Jesus stuff is not so hot." The disciples are embarrassed by their public failure. Instead of caring for this man and his son, they get into a big religious argument and grow defensive: "You're wrong and we're right!" The big fight is entertaining the crowd.

Jesus walks up and surveys the scene. He asks what is going on: "What are you arguing about?"

The father tells Jesus how his son is tormented by a spirit that has made him mute and throws him to the ground in convulsions. He adds, "I brought him hoping you could help, but you were gone, so I asked your disciples to help me. I must have gotten some of the disciples in the remedial class, because they haven't been able to do a thing."

The disciples are staring at their feet. This is not a shining moment for them. They lack spiritual power and have failed to help someone in need. Moreover, they ended up in a big fight that was doing no good at all and looked ridiculous to the crowd of onlookers.

Sometimes one of the biggest obstacles to faith in Jesus is the incompetence, complacency, and arrogance of his followers— followers like me.

Jesus says, "O unbelieving generation, how long shall I stay with you?" (Mark 9:19). Mostly he's talking about his disciples. He says to the father, "Bring me your boy," and the father does so. The boy goes into violent convulsions and rolls around on the floor, foaming at the mouth. Everybody is very quiet now. Jesus asks, "How long has he been like this?" The dad says, "A long time—from childhood. A lot of times he's nearly died."

Then the father requests, "But if you can do anything, take pity on us and help us" (Mark 9:22). Sometimes what we really believe—our core convictions—leak out of us in a single word. And so it was with this man.

If.

If is not a mountaintop word. It is valley talk. *If.*

"Jesus, this is my boy. I pray to God for him every day. For years I've told God, 'God, I'll do anything. I'll give you anything. I'll promise you anything.' Nothing ... nothing.

"Jesus, every time a new rabbi came around, every time there was a teacher, every time there was a holy man with a reputation for healing and spiritual power, I'd bring my son to him. I'd ask him, 'Can you do anything to help us?' The answer was nothing ... nothing.

"Then I heard about you, and I got my hopes up. Do you know how much it hurts to get your hopes up, Jesus? I got my hopes up one more time, and I brought my boy to your disciples, and it turned into a circus. That's my boy, and it's like a freak show with everybody looking at him. But if you could do anything ..."

Jesus picks up on this word "if," and we read this amazing statement that gives us hope and then slays us: "Everything is possible for him who believes" (Mark 9:23). Jesus, in a way, is coming back with an *if* of his own. The man says help me if it's possible. Jesus says all things are possible—*if* you believe.

There's power in faith, in interacting with spiritual reality. Jesus believes this.

At this point, if I had been the father, I'd have been tempted to conjure up some certainty, or to fake it. "Oops—did I say 'if'? I meant 'since'—'since you can do anything.'" For the giants of faith use prepositions that link the certainty of their beliefs to their confidence in fulfillment: *since, therefore, because*." Not *if*.

But this man has iffy faith and prays an iffy prayer. When Jesus points this out, a response comes out of this man's mouth so fast that it is like an eruption, because this is exactly his quandary. His

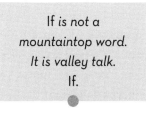

If *is not a mountaintop word. It is valley talk.* If.

hope dangles by a slender *if*. Immediately the boy's father exclaims, "I do believe; help me overcome my unbelief!" (Mark 9:24).

I believe and I doubt. I hope and I fear. I pray and I waver. I ask and I worry. I believe; help my unbelief.

I get that prayer. That's the Doubter's Prayer. Take away my *if*. I believe; help my unbelief.

Now this is not exactly a ringing endorsement of Jesus, and you wonder, "How is he going to respond?"

Jesus says, "I'm shocked and appalled you actually have doubts. Too bad for you.... I have no time for this kind of insulting request!" (Reversions 9:25; I just kind of made that one up).

Aren't you glad Jesus doesn't really say that? Aren't you glad he doesn't walk away? Instead, he speaks to the man's son. The boy is healed and will live. He will grow up. He will make friends. He will learn the Torah. He will work alongside his dad. He will get married someday, maybe. He will grow to be an old, old man, and he will remember the day when he was a boy and a young rabbi did what nobody else could do. He will remember the day he stood alone with Jesus on a mountain.

Beyond the Mountain

Now the question is: How about us? Do you think this story really happened? Maybe you have doubts. Maybe you wonder about the demon thing. Maybe you wonder if miracles are really possible. Maybe your faith is filled with *if*.

There is a wonderful, tiny verse in a rarely read New Testament letter called Jude: "Be merciful to those who doubt" (v. 22). Jesus understands our *ifs*. The dad in this story had at least as much doubt as you do — at least that much doubt.

Yet something inside cannot quit hoping. Something inside keeps drawing us back to this rabbi. Something about his life, his works, his faith. Something about his belief that the universe is run by the kind of Father Jesus described and loved. Something about his power. Something about his peace draws us to him as it has drawn people all over the world to him for two thousand years and draws them still.

> We can't see and know everything about hope now, but one day we will.

Something deep inside tells you that you are standing alone on the edge of a cliff, and the only alternative to Jesus is illusion or despair.

We can't see and know everything about hope now, but one day we will. Maybe it's like this, as written by a preacher named Bruce Thielemann:

The Leap

Imagine a colony of grubs living on the bottom of a swamp. And every once in a while, one of these grubs is inclined to climb a leaf stem to the surface. Then he disappears above the surface and never returns. All the grubs wonder why this is so and what it must be like up there, so they counsel among themselves and agree that the next one who goes up will come back and tell the others. Not long after that, one of the grubs feels the urge and climbs that leaf stem and goes out above the surface onto a lily pad. And there in the warmth of the sun, he falls asleep. While he sleeps, the carapace of the tiny creature breaks open, and out of the inside of the grub comes a magnificent dragonfly with beautiful, wide, rainbow-hued, iridescent wings. And he spreads those wings and flies, soaring out over those waters. But then he remembers the commitment he has made to those behind, yet now he knows he cannot return. They would not recognize him in the first place, and beyond that, he could not live again in such a place. But one thought of his takes away all the distress: they, too, shall climb the stem, and they, too, shall know the glory.

One day, the Bible says, it will happen. One day our grubby little *if* will become a glorious *when*.

Maybe you're standing on the side of the cliff, stuck on *if*; wondering, "Can I entrust myself to him? Can I commit myself even though I doubt? If I take a leap, will he catch me?"

It really does not matter what I write, because no one can or should try to talk anyone else into this. But I know something about how *if* works. I know that if you never believe, if you never trust, you will never know. Sometimes a leap of faith is the only form of transportation.

One other thing I know. I know about the secret hope you've been hoping for.

EVERYBODY HOPES

Creatures are not born with desires
unless satisfaction for those desires exists.

C. S. LEWIS

We all are hopers. We are creatures who cannot stop wishing. We are four-leaf-clover collectors. We wish on the evening star. We tell stories about genies coming out of a bottle to grant three wishes. After a turkey dinner, my cousin Danny and I used to grab the ends of the wishbone from the turkey and break it in the belief that whoever got the longer piece would get his wish. Where that came from I have no idea. The bone didn't do the turkey much good.

We teach our children to make a wish before blowing out the candle. When my children were small, they loved the movie *Pinnochio*; especially they loved a plucky, chirpy, irrepressible character named Jiminy Cricket. If you go to the Magic Kingdom at Disneyland, the "happiest place on earth," you can still hear him sing, "When you wish upon a star ..."

We all hope. There is even an anonymous online wish list where people by the thousands record what they're hoping for—some of the entries are funny, some are scary, and some are heartrending. "I wish to be rich in the immediate future." "I wish to be very happy because every aspect of my life is going fantastically well forever." "I wish my wife would die." "I wish it wasn't pancreatic." Many of the wishes are followed by the word *please*. We just can't help ourselves. George MacDonald has said, "Anything large enough for a wish to light upon, is large enough to hang a prayer upon."

We all hope, but hope comes in two flavors: hoping *for something* and hoping *in someone*. Now, when we are hoping for something, we are hoping for a particular outcome. "I hope I get that job. I hope I get that house. I hope I get that girl. I hope I get that girl and she gets that job and we get that house." Sometimes the thing we hope for is life or death: "I hope this depression lifts." "I hope it's not cancer." But one day it will be. If not cancer, it will be something else.

One day—and this is the truth—every *thing* we hope for will eventually disappoint us. Every circumstance, every situation that we hope *for* is going to wear out, give out, fall apart, melt down, go away. When that happens, the question then is about your deeper hope, your foundational hope, your fallback hope when all your other hopes are disappointed.

Hoping can break your heart. The difference between hoping and wishing, says writer William Sessions, is the presence of strong desire. In the movie *The Shawshank Redemption*, the two central characters, played by Tim Robbins and Morgan Freeman, have a running argument about hope. Morgan Freeman has learned to manage disappointment by giving up hope. "Hope is a dangerous thing," he says. "Hope can break your heart." To Tim Robbins, though, to quit hoping is to start dying. And the final line of the movie, as Morgan Freeman has left prison and headed for the blue waters of Mexico and the reunion with his great good friend, is "I hope . . ."

Hoping can break your heart. That is why we carry one big hope, the secret hope you don't even dare to breathe: that when you have lost the *something* you were hoping *for*, and it might have been really, really big, there is a *Someone* you can put your hope *in*.

The whole testimony of the Scriptures points to this one Man, points to a God, not because he will be able to give us this *thing* or that *thing* we were hoping *for* — because that's always going to give out eventually — but because he is the *one* we can put our hope *in*. And without hope, as Pope John Paul II once said, there is no faith. Hope is faith waiting for tomorrow. Faith requires belief, and believing is what we do with our minds. Faith requires commitment, and committing is what we do with our wills. But faith must also have hope, and hoping is what we do in our hearts.

Wishful Thinking

The Old Testament records a story of believers and skeptics and an early atheist. The story takes place early on in the history of Israel, after the Israelites have been wandering around in the desert for forty years carrying the ark of the covenant with them. They get to the Promised Land, but they are struggling. They don't have a king; this is before the time of David and Solomon. Israel is fighting against the Philistines, and they are hoping for *something*, hoping for victory. They go into a battle with the Philistines, and they lose. Afterward they debrief, and they ask what happened. This often happens with people. They ask, "Where was God? We were counting on him. Why didn't he give us what we were hoping for?"

Then somebody gets an idea and says, "Let's go into battle with the Philistines again; only this time we'll use our secret weapon. This time we'll bring the ark of the covenant into the battle."

The ark of the covenant was a box in which the Israelites kept some of the manna (the bread God had provided during their time in the wilderness) and the Ten Commandments. But it was not just a box. It represented the "presence of God." They were thinking about it as "God in a box." If they brought it into battle, God wouldn't let the enemy capture the ark of the covenant. It would be like capturing God, and he wasn't going to let that happen. They thought, *Then he has to give us what we're hoping for.*

There is an odd kind of theology behind this way of thinking. I'll give you a picture of it. In one episode of the animated television show *The Simpsons*, Homer pledges money to a PBS telethon fund drive because he's tired of the fund drive, but he doesn't actually have the money. When the PBS people find out about it, they force him to serve with a group of missionaries on a tropical island. The people he's serving with build a new church. Now, Homer is not a theologically astute character, but he's proud of their accomplishment. He sums it up like this: "Well, I don't know much about God, but we sure have built him a nice little cage."

But the truth about God is that you just can't keep him in a cage. He can't be tamed or domesticated. You can't force him to give you the *thing* you are hoping *for*.

That is what the Israelites try to do. They go into battle a second time, and it's a disaster. Their army is crushed. They lose seven times more soldiers in the second battle than they did the first time around. Worst of all for them, the ark of the covenant is captured.

This is unthinkable. To lose the ark is to lose the presence of God. It is to lose what makes them distinct as a people. Their priest and his two sons die; and the priest's daughter-in-law is in labor when she gets the news. She names her son *Ichabod* then dies herself.

Chabod was a beautiful word to Israel. It meant glory. Putting an *I* in front of it made it a negative (like *atheist* is the opposite of *theist*). She wanted her son to know what she perceived as the truth and not to look for comfort in a delusion. There was no God.

No meaning. No hope. No glory. Ichabod. She wanted to warn her son that wishing does not make something so. Hope can break one's heart.

Many people believe in an Ichabod world—that faith is nothing more than wishful thinking. We'd like to believe we will live after we die; we'd like to think there is a benevolent all-powerful being in the sky, so we talk ourselves into it.

No one has named our modern world Ichabod more powerfully than Sigmund Freud. Freud said that we each are made up of the id, the ego, and the superego (think of the Three Stooges: the id is Curly—all appetite and fun and chasing blond nurses; the ego is Larry—relatively tame and bland and accepting of reality; the superego is Moe—always bossing people around and poking them in the eye). Wishing is the fundamental characteristic of infancy, dominated by the id. The main sign of maturity in Freud is realizing that wishing is powerless before reality. And, Freud said, the biggest illusion of wishful thinking that human beings ever dream up is God. He wrote a book about religion called *The Future of an Illusion*. It is better, he said, to grow up out of our wishful thinking.

> *The ark of the covenant was not just a box. It represented the "presence of God." They were thinking about it as "God in a box." The Israelites thought,* he has to give us what we're hoping for.

Maybe Freud is right. But one problem with Freud's line of thought is that it cuts both ways. Someone may become a doubter out of wishful thinking as well. C. S. Lewis said his greatest wish was that there not be a God, that he be left alone. He said that speaking of man's search for God always sounded to him like speaking of the mouse's search for the cat.

Psychiatrist and researcher Paul Vitz, in his book *Faith of the Fatherless*, argues that no empirical research supports the idea that faith is neurotic; but a whole mountain of it says that faith is healthy. This suggests that perhaps it is atheism that requires a psychological explanation. In fact, when Vitz traces the backgrounds of many major atheists versus major theists of recent centuries, he finds that those drawn to atheism are overwhelmingly more likely to come from a background with a weak, abusive, or absent father.

The term "wishful thinking" usually carries negative connotations. We normally use it to refer to those who childishly allow what they want to be true to override logic and reason. However, there is another way to use the phrase: we can think about our wishes. We can ask whether perhaps our wishes tell us something true about why we exist and what we were made for.

This is how Frederick Buechner uses the phrase. "Christianity is mainly wishful thinking. Even the part about Judgment and Hell reflects the wish that somewhere the score is being kept.... Sometimes wishing is the wings the truth comes true on. Sometimes the truth is what sets us wishing for it."

Someone to Hope *In*

Getting back to our story of the Israelites and the ark of the covenant, we find the people of Israel desperate. But it is when they have lost everything they have been hoping *for* that the story gets interesting. The Philistines carry the ark of the covenant off to the city of Ashdod where the temple of their god Dagon is located. The priests take the ark inside and place it next to the statue of Dagon. Then all the Philistines cheer, because they believe that Dagon has prevailed over Yahweh, the God of the Israelites. They have a big feast, chant their favorite chants, tell their battle stories. Then night falls and everybody goes home. No one is present to see or hear what is going on, and something happens in the temple.

"When the people of Ashdod rose early the next day, there was Dagon, fallen on his face on the ground before the ark of the LORD!" (1 Samuel 5:3). The text does not tell us what the priests thought. Maybe Dagon falling down was an accident. Maybe it was just a coincidence. But it looks suspiciously as if Dagon has bowed down to worship the God of Israel. It looks as if maybe the God of Israel is the Lord of Lords.

Dagon's priests realize that it does not look good to have their god bowing down to the God of Israel, Yahweh, so they dust their god off and prop him back up. All day long, on the second day, Philistines come into the temple to celebrate their victory and offer sacrifices and sing songs to the great Dagon. Then night falls, and the priests turn off the lights and go home. They leave Dagon alone with the great Yahweh. Dagon says to himself, "Here we go again."

The next morning when they come in, the priests find that once more Dagon has fallen on the ground before the ark of the Lord. Not only that, but this time his head and his hands have been cut off and laid neatly across the threshold of the temple, and all that was left of Dagon inside the temple was a stump.

A Three-Day Story

Wouldn't you love to know what happened? The text doesn't tell us. All we know is that this is a "three-day story." The first day is a very dark day. It looks as if the God of Israel is defeated and the glory is gone. In fact, there is a very poignant episode. After they lose the battle and the ark is captured and the old priest Eli dies, his daughter, the old new atheist, names her son *Ichabod*. "The whole thing is a pipe dream. Abraham was deluded. Moses was just wandering around in the wilderness. There is no God, no Yahweh. No glory. Life doesn't mean anything. You're born. You die. That's it. Our son may as well know that as soon as he's grown up. Ichabod. Glory's gone." That's the first day. Heaven is silent. No hope. No glory. No one can understand why. Some days are like that.

Then there is the second day, a day of hidden combat. It is shrouded in mystery. It is the day Dagon falls down but gets propped back up. It is a day of ambiguity and anxiety. Some days are like that.

But this is a third-day story. On the third day, the story takes a 180-degree turn. The idol is overturned. The time of captivity is over. God is going to come home to his people because the third day is God's day. That's the day of hope. He's the "third-day God." This part of the story gets a little earthy—I would apologize for it, but it comes out of the text. God sent a plague that involved mice.

What the Philistines are afflicted with is hard to translate: The New International Version has "tumors," kind of a polite choice. The Modern Language Bible is a little more literal: "The Lord's hand lay heavy on the Ashdodites. He punished them with hemorrhoids, both at Ashdod and in its suburbs" (1 Samuel 5:6). The King James Version is just slightly more delicate: "they had hemorrhoids in their secret parts" (5:9; that's where they usually go). The obvious question is, why would this detail make it into the Bible? What got into whoever was writing this material?

> The Philistines—Israel's enemies—were very powerful; they had Iron Age technology. But in the presence of God's judgment, the Philistines were embarrassingly human.

This detail is a very deliberate part of the story—here's why. These were the Philistines—Israel's enemies. There were very powerful; they had Iron Age technology. The writer wants the readers to know: Don't be afraid of your enemies. Don't envy them. Don't try to be like them.

If for a while it looked like the Philistines were going to come out on top, don't be deceived. That was first-day stuff. Third day was coming.

The writer wants us to know that in the presence of God's judgment, the Philistines were embarrassingly human. All their iron swords, spears, and shields did them no good, because what they really needed was inflatable cushions to sit on, and while the Iron Age had arrived, the Inflatable Cushion Age was still centuries away.

One of the ways you can divide up Bible stories is by their time frame. One kind of story is the forty-day story. These are usually "wait-around-and-learn-patience" stories. Noah's family was in the ark for forty days and nights of rain; the Israelites hung around Mount Sinai forty days waiting for the Ten Commandments; Elijah spent forty days in the wilderness hiding out from Jezebel. Jesus began his ministry by spending forty days in the wilderness; after the resurrection he and the disciples spent another forty days waiting for his ascension and then the coming of the Holy Spirit. The focus of these stories is on the need for people to be faithful, to persevere. Forty-day stories are Crock-Pot stories.

But there is another kind of story: the three-day story. These are stories about crisis and urgency—microwave stories. The focus here is not on the need for a human response at all. Here the pressure is so crushing that God must show up to rescue—or it's curtains. Three-day stories are stories of desperate need and anticipation and hope hanging by a thread.

When a hero named Joseph was in prison, he said to Pharaoh's cupbearer, "Within three days Pharaoh will lift up your head and restore you to your position" (Genesis 40:13).

When Israel was trapped in slavery, Moses asked Pharaoh, "Let us take a three-day journey into the desert" (Exodus 5:3).

When the Israelites arrive at Sinai, God said, "Go to the people and consecrate them today and tomorrow.... And be ready the third day, because on that day the LORD will come down on Mount Sinai in the sight of all the people" (Exodus 19:10–11).

When Israel was afraid to go into the Promised Land, God said to Israel, "Be strong and courageous.... Three days from now you will cross the Jordan here to go in and take possession of the land the LORD your God is giving you for your own" (Joshua 1:6, 11).

When Israel was threatened with genocide, Queen Esther said that she would fast for three days then go to the king to seek deliverance for her people.

Want to take a guess on how long Jonah was in the belly of the big fish? Yep, he was in there three days before he was released. His prayer the whole time he was in that big fish was, "God, just let me go out the way I came in." At least I think that's probably what his prayer was.

The third day was used so frequently in this way that it became kind of a technical expression meaning a time to wait for deliverance. "Right now, things are messed up. Right now, hope is being crushed. Right now, hearts are disappointed. But a better day is coming."

In the book of Hosea, the prophet says it like this: "Come, let us return to the LORD.... After two days, he will revive us; on the third day he will restore us, that we may live in his presence" (Hosea 6:1–2).

Be Careful What You Hope For

One day deliverance came in a way that nobody was looking for. God came back to his people, not in a box, but in a man. "The Word became flesh," the Bible says, "and dwelt among us" (John 1:14 NASB). This language is very evocative. The word for *dwelt* literally is the word used for "tabernacle" — "tabernacled [tented] among us." Because the tabernacle was the place where the ark of the covenant was, that was where the Israelites thought of God being.

"The Word became flesh, and dwelt [tabernacled] among us, and we saw His glory [his *chabod*], glory as of the only begotten from the Father" (John 1:14 NASB). But it was a funny kind of glory. It came in a strange combination of humility, loneliness, and fearlessness. Nobody could tame Jesus. Nobody—not the politicians, not the Zealots, not the religious leaders—nobody could use him. Nobody could manipulate him to get what they wanted. Nobody could shut him up. So in the end, those who were in power took him and lashed him with a whip and pierced him with a sword and hung him on a cross. Then his body was laid in a tomb.

That was the first day—a dark day. His followers were crushed. They had seen the glory for a while, and now it was gone. Now it was lying in a tomb. Now it was Ichabod.

The second day, it didn't look any better. On the second day, Pontius Pilate posted a guard to stand watch over the tomb, because he was in control now. He wanted to make sure that nothing happened—nobody came in and did anything funny with that body. He said to himself, "Well, I guess that's the end of that. I guess we won't hear any more about that movement. I don't know much about this Jesus, but we sure have built him a nice little cage."

> *The thing about Jesus is that you just can't keep him in a cage. He never was a cage kind of guy. The authorities didn't know it, but death wasn't defeat for him.*

But the thing about Jesus is that you just can't keep him in a cage. He never was a cage kind of guy. The authorities didn't know it, but death wasn't defeat for him. He died, we're told, "for our sins." He died to do what you and I, with all our little efforts at self-improvement—trying to do better, give enough, go to church enough, do enough nice things—could never do. He was setting everything right between God and us. He was dying the death that, by all rights, you and I should have died.

That was the second day. That was a dark day. That was a disappointing day.

But the story of Jesus is a three-day story.

Some people maintain that the third day never happened. Jesus was never raised. His body is still lying in a cave someplace. A recent documentary produced by James Cameron (the *Titanic* producer) called *The Lost Tomb of Jesus* suggests that Jesus' body was never raised. The basis for Cameron's thesis was that a tomb with several ossuaries in it had been found in Jerusalem. Death in the ancient world was a two-stage process. When someone died, the body was placed in a tomb or a cave. Then, after a period of time, the bones would be collected and put in a box called an ossuary.

One of the ossuaries in this particular tomb had the name "Joseph" inscribed on it; one of them had the name "Mary"; and one of them may have had the name "Jesus," but the name was a little hard to decrypt. The documentary claims that these ossuaries indicate that Jesus was never resurrected and that the third day never happened. This is a very important thing, because faith hinges on this third day.

Interestingly, scholars have actually known about the tomb since its discovery in 1980. None of the scholars involved, Christian or not, thought there was even a remote chance that it was the tomb of the family of Jesus of Nazareth, partly because the names were so common in first-century Jerusalem. Tom Wright, a New Testament scholar, says that they are so common that finding a tomb with those names on the ossuaries would be much like finding a New York phone directory with the names John and Sally Smith in it. Nine hundred tombs have been found around Jerusalem over the last century or so, and numbers of them contain ossuaries that are labeled "Jesus, son of Joseph."

Furthermore, the Joseph in the Bible lived in Nazareth. He never lived in Jerusalem and certainly wouldn't have been buried there.

What's more, the tombs of martyrs in Jesus' day were always venerated. They were visited by the followers of the martyrs, and their sites became destinations for pilgrimages. If Jesus had a known tomb, it would have been venerated by his followers and would have kept anyone from claiming he had been raised from the dead. Moreover, we have written documentation within one generation of Jesus' life, when there were still eyewitnesses around to challenge it, that five hundred people saw him alive again after his resurrection.

The list of evidence against that tomb being the place where Jesus' bones are has gotten so long that the latest rumor is that skeptics are claiming this is the "true tomb of Jesus" because they found a bracelet in it that said, "What would I do?" (I don't think that rumor is true.)

The followers of Jesus made a claim: "You know, the first day was a real dark day. That's the day they laid him in the tomb. The second day the guard was posted. That was a real dark day. We thought it was done. We thought that the thing that we were hoping for was never going to come true. What we found out was that there was someone we could hope in. That was way better news than anything we were hoping for. Because of him, the third day came."

The third day is God's day. The third day is the day when prisoners of Pharaoh get set free. The third day is the day when the people come to the mountains and the mountains shake and rivers are parted and people go into the Promised Land. The third day is the day when harem girls like Esther face down powerful kings.

The third day is the day when prophets like Jonah are dropped off at seaside ports by giant fish. The third day is the day when idols like Dagon come tumbling down and God starts coming home to his people. The third day is the day stones are rolled away.

The third day is the day a crucified carpenter came back to life.

You never know what God is going to do, because God is "God of the third day."

I know. It's a hope, not a proof. But is a lesser hope worth hoping for?

In the early twentieth century a hobo named Cliff Edwards was barely staying alive, but he pinned his hopes on his one great gift — a voice that could slide up three octaves with pure quicksilver magic. He started singing at a restaurant where he billed himself as "Ukelele Ike," got discovered, and became one of the great vaudeville and Broadway stars of the 1920s as well as a star of early talkie movies. He was as big as a person came. He is credited in some circles with inventing scat singing. And if you picture a 1920s singer carrying a ukulele, you are venerating his memory.

> You never know what God is going to do, because God is "God of the third day."

Edwards got what he hoped for, but it wasn't what he wanted. And he began the long slide down — alcoholism, gambling, tax troubles, bankruptcy, and drug addiction. He died forgotten, broke, and on welfare in 1971; he outlived Janis Joplin and Jimi Hendrix and his own fame by many decades. I have a soft spot for him because of the last big movie part he got before his long, final descent — when his inimitable voice gave life to the role of a plucky, chirpy, irrepressible character named Jiminy Cricket. "When you wish upon a star ..."

It is a matter of historical record that once there was a time when a little band of frightened, foolish men and women said, "We don't know how it happened, but the third day came." The third day is the only explanation for how that little band of faltering men and women became this church in which people would, without fear, be hung on crosses, be pierced with swords, give up their lives.

If it were not true ... if the third day had not come ... if anybody could have pointed to a pile of bones, they would have pointed.

Nobody is going to die for a pile of bones, but for a third-day God, people would give their lives because of what lies on the other side of the third day.

From that third day on, the world has never been the same. Jesus' followers, who used to observe the Sabbath, began instead to observe on Sunday—on the third day—what they began to call, in the New Testament, the "Lord's Day." The third day is the Lord's Day, because, they said, "we're third-day people now. We're betting the farm on this one." They said that the kingdom they all had longed for turned out to be real.

You never know what might happen on the third day. I cling to that. I put all my hope in a third-day God.

But I live in a second-day world.

The Strange Silence of God

We may cry out with longing and despair to the cold uncaring universe ...
but we will only hear silence in return. The universe is mute, devoid
of all power to either affirm or deny the worth we place on either
ourselves or on others. So be it. We do not matter to the universe.

Kenneth A. Taylor

I spent six years of my life in graduate school getting a PhD in clinical psychology. I was a therapist once, briefly, and I will tell you about my first suicide.

For those who do professional counseling, suicide is their worst nightmare. It is probed for in the initial intake: "Have you ever thought of hurting yourself? If you did, have you ever thought about how? If you did, have you ever actually tried?" I took a whole class devoted to it: who is most at risk; what the breakdown is by gender, age, and profession; what the signs are that it might be imminent; how to form an action plan; and what the legal issues are.

To make things worse, I was not a good counselor. Strong, dynamic leaders will sometimes confess their shortcomings as counselors: "I just tell people to straighten up. I'm too strong, too directive, too impatient...." That wasn't my problem. I just found that far too often I didn't know what to say.

My first experience in counseling was when I took a class in client-centered therapy, rooted in the work of psychologist Carl Rogers. The idea in client-centered therapy is that you don't give advice and you don't ask questions; you simply rephrase what the client says with empathy and congruence to help him or her reach a deeper place. My problem was that my first client came against her will because her husband had signed her up. (Since we were student counselors, the sessions were free.)

After we had met, she said to me, "So why am I here?" A tape recorder was running, and I knew my supervisor would listen to the session. I was supposed to follow the rules. "I hear you wondering what you're doing here," I said empathically.

"Yes," she said, "what are we supposed to do?"

"My sense is that you're curious about where things go from here...."

Things went downhill from there, and she quit a few sessions later.

It was several years later during an internship at a psychiatric clinic that I was assigned a client I'll call Claire. She was in her late twenties, a year older than me, and had more experience receiving therapy than I had giving it. She came with a thick folder and had previously been diagnosed as what was called a borderline personality as well as with depression.

I simply was not prepared for the litany of pain that was her life and background. She did not know her biological father. Her mother was mentally ill and an alcoholic and would sometimes threaten to kill her and weep and proclaim her love for her in the same paragraph. She had a stepfather who took her into his bed when she was eight years old. Her grandfather did the same thing a few years later. So did her uncle.

Claire could not hold a job or sustain a friendship. She deserved much better help than I could give her, but she could not afford to pay for it, and because I had not finished my degree, I worked at a clinic with a sliding scale. She would sometimes be unable to speak for twenty or thirty minutes at a stretch. She had attempted suicide so many times that her wrists had scars that from a distance looked like bracelets. Her need for contact, for reassurance that someone knew she was alive, was omnivorous. Working with a borderline personality in therapy is much like trying to save a drowning person who is lost in panic.

> We talked about God sometimes. She knew I believed. And she wanted to. But she wondered why no one heard—or if Someone did hear, why he didn't answer.

We talked about God sometimes. She knew I believed. And she wanted to. But she could remember praying, when she was a little girl, that she would not have to go back in that bedroom. And she wondered why no one heard—or if Someone did hear, why he didn't answer.

I believe—deeply, passionately—that lives can change. But I tend to believe this abstractly, as an idea. I did not have much faith that Claire could change through what we would do together. There are many debates in clinical outcome research about what makes therapy effective, but one of the seminal ideas that psychotherapist Jerome Frank wrote of in a book called *Persuasion and Healing* is that the critical issue is whether the healer has faith that healing will happen. When faith is present, amazing results can occur. This is behind, for instance, the whole "placebo effect," which is widely verified. This is the faith I did not have.

But someone had it for me. I was receiving weekly supervision from a veteran psychiatrist whom I'll call Dana. He was a widower, a tall, white-haired sage who had studied in Vienna. He was Yoda and Merlin and Dr. Phil rolled into one, a gentle, quiet man, and as good a listener as I have ever known. I was seeing many clients, but because Claire's case was so severe, most of our time was spent talking about her.

I learned empathy from Dana. I had never seen anyone internalize a client's world like he did. I can still remember how he told me that twenty years earlier, when his wife died of cancer, he left his pictures of her in his office in their old places and did not speak of her death to his clients. He did not want his more fragile clients to have to feel a sense of change or loss in what was for some of them the only safe place in their lives. He did not want to add to their burdens.

He listened, with sad eyes, to Claire's story. He was a believer in God and spoke of how he would pray for the clients who came to him. He cared. And through him, I cared better too. We developed a plan to help her. It was very modest since I would be seeing her for only that one year of graduate school. One of our goals was simply that she be able to make it through the year without any suicidal gestures.

Claire and I finished our year together, and I moved to another rotation. She was assigned to another low-cost trainee. I do not know what happened to her. I would like to think that she gained confidence, found a reason to live, maybe even got married.

But I know what happened to Dana. One Saturday morning the police department responded to a note in their mail by rushing to Dana's garage and forcing the door open and finding his body in the car, which had been running through the night. Dana had left the note in their mailbox late the night before. He wanted to make sure he was found over the weekend so that his clients could be notified about what had happened and not surprised by coming to the office and finding him absent.

I don't know what inside Dana made him think that life wasn't worth it, that God couldn't change it. Maybe the pain of carrying so much sadness was more than he could bear. Maybe he tried too much to carry it alone. Maybe he had bad genes; maybe his neurons fired too slowly, and if they had been helped along, he never would have left life the way he did. Maybe he soldiered on for years in a battle against pain far more heroic than any I will ever fight.

But I know Dana cared more and better than I did. I know he wanted to help in ways that were more unseen and unapplauded than mine.

I don't know why God didn't do more to help him.

Devil's Advocate

I want to look at this "strange silence of God." I want to examine as honestly as I can why some aspects of life cause us to doubt. The medieval church used to hire a lawyer to make the case against anyone proposed for sainthood. This lawyer was called a "devil's advocate." His purpose was to give decisions integrity. Honest doubt is the devil's advocate that honest faith requires. Let's listen to some of that doubt.

We who are believers find that we live in the same world as those among us who are unbelievers. We see the same circumstances that unbelievers see. We thrill over the same sunsets and agonize over the same multitudes of unfed children. Like unbelievers, most of the believers I know do not claim to have seen visions; we don't hear voices; we don't experience the kind of miracles that could prove God in some scientific, demonstrable way. Like unbelievers, those of us who believe are troubled by the same evil and pain in the world and by the same suffering in our own lives. Like them, we too are often disappointed in Christians. Like them, we are disappointed by the lack of progress in our own lives and growth.

Yet some of us choose to believe in and bet our entire existence on a God we cannot see, cannot touch, cannot hear, and cannot prove. Others choose to bet their entire existence on the notion that such a God does not exist.

I will tell you about the doubts that trouble me. My doubts—at least the big ones, the major league doubts—can be put in three categories. One category involves the lack of evidence. I wish sometimes that there could be the same kind of proof for the existence of God that there is for the existence of Italy or the chicken pox.

> Some of us choose to believe in and bet our entire existence on a God we cannot see, touch, hear, or prove. Others choose to bet their entire existence on the notion that such a God does not exist.

A second category involves believers themselves. Why aren't we better people? If what Jesus said is true, why doesn't God say something about his followers engaging in crusades and inquisitions and witch burning and church-sanctioned slavery? And why can some Christians be negative, judgmental, hypocritical, and even uncaring to those in our society who we think are unlike us?

The third category is the problem of pain. Why must there be such awful suffering? Why does it strike so needlessly and randomly without explanation? Why doesn't God explain what's going on—or better yet, put an end to it?

So we will let doubt speak, and I'll say a bit about why I think these doubts do not get the last word. But I might as well tell you now that I still have questions about them. We will come to the main reason why I have faith in another chapter, but it is not because I have conclusive answers to God's strange silence.

1. Why Not More Proof?

If God is there, why doesn't he make more noise? If believing in God is such a big deal to him, why doesn't God make himself more obvious? Why doesn't he just part the clouds and write his name in the sky? Why doesn't he give us more compelling proof and evidence? Is he an introvert? Does he just, like Greta Garbo, want to be alone?

One of the most famous atheists in the last century was Bertrand Russell. When he was ninety years old, he had a famous encounter with a woman at a party. The woman said to him, "Mr. Russell, you are not only the world's most famous atheist; you are maybe the world's oldest atheist. You will die soon. What will you do if, after you die, it turns out that God exists? What will you do if you come face-to-face with this God whom you've defied your whole life long?"

Bertrand Russell responded to her that he would point his finger at God and say, "You, sir, gave us insufficient evidence."

Woody Allen had a more concrete suggestion. He said he'd believe in God if God would just give him an unmistakable sign, like making a large deposit in a Swiss bank account in Woody's name.

An atheist philosopher named Norwood Russell Hanson said, "I'm not a stubborn guy. I would become a theist, a believer, under some conditions. I'm open-minded." Then he went on to lay out the conditions under which he would believe:

[Suppose] next Tuesday morning, just after breakfast, all of us in this one world [are] knocked to our knees by a percussive and ear-shattering thunderclap. Snow swirls, leaves drop from trees, the earth heaves and buckles, buildings topple and towers tumble. The sky is ablaze with an eerie silvery light, and just then, as all the people of this world look up, the heavens open, and the clouds pull apart, revealing an unbelievably radiant and immense Zeus-like figure towering over us like a hundred Everests. He frowns darkly as lightning plays over the features of his Michelangeloid face, and then he points down, at me, and explains for every man, woman, and child to hear, "I've had quite enough of your too-clever logic chopping and word-watching in matters of theology. *Be assured, Norwood Russell Hanson, that I most certainly do exist!*"

Yes, I think that would get my attention too. It would be enough to have a vision of a God with Michelangeloid features, but to have him give you the middle name treatment would be a head-turner, no doubt about it.

I often fantasize that having a powerful mystical encounter would settle all faith issues once and for all. But for people who have them, it doesn't seem to work that way. Sometimes people come to the mountain, hear the thunder, see the smoke and lightning, and a few months later they are bellyaching about having to camp in the wilderness and whining about how they want to go back to Egypt and slavery for the leeks and onions. Maybe God has his reasons for the silence.

I think of Agnes. From the time she was a young girl, Agnes believed. Not just believed—she was on fire. She wanted to do great things for God. She said she wanted to "love Jesus as he has never been loved before." She knew Jesus was with her and had an undeniable sense of him calling her. She wrote in her journal, "My soul at present is in perfect peace and joy." She experienced a union with God that was so deep and so continual that it was to her a rapture. She left her home, became a missionary, gave him everything.

And then God left her.

At least, that is how it felt to her. *Where is my faith?* she wondered. *Even deep down there is nothing but emptiness and darkness. . . . My God, how painful is this unknown pain. . . . I have no faith.* She tried to pray: "I utter words of community prayers—and try my utmost to get out of every word the sweetness it has to give. But my prayer of union is not there any longer. I no longer pray."

On the outside she worked, she served, she smiled. But she spoke of her smile as her "mask, a cloak that covers everything."

This inner darkness and dryness and pain over the absence of God continued on, year after year, with one brief respite, for nearly fifty years. Such was the secret pain of Agnes, who is better known as Mother Teresa.

The letters that expressed her inner torment were a secret during her life, and she asked that they be destroyed. But a strange thing has happened. Her willingness to persist in the face of such agonizing doubts brings comfort and strength to people that an inner life of ease and certainty never could. As in her life she was a servant of the poor, so in her anguish she has become a missionary for those who doubt.

How are we to understand this? It should warn us about easy formulas that are guaranteed to make us feel closer to God. There is an old saying, "If you don't feel close to God anymore—who moved?" That might have been a good question for Nathan to ask David after Bathsheba-gate. But I wouldn't have wanted to ask that of Mother Teresa.

Some people, of course, see this as Mother Teresa just butting up against the reality that God isn't really there after all. "She was no more exempt from the realization that religion is a human fabrication than any other person, and that her attempted cure was more and more professions of faith could only have deepened the pit that she had dug for herself," writes Christopher Hitchens. Richard Dawkins warned everyone not to be "taken in by the sanctimoniously hypocritical Mother Teresa." This, by the way, strikes me as bad strategy. If you are trying to convert people to atheism, taking a shot at Mother Teresa can't be your best move.

> *Having a powerful mystical encounter would settle all faith issues once and for all. But for people who have them, it doesn't seem to work that way. Maybe God has his reasons for the silence.*

But Mother Teresa didn't have this negative understanding. She did not reject God, but neither did she overcome her pain over God's silence. Rather, in a strange way, it became a part of her. A wise spiritual counselor told her three things she needed to hear. One was that there was no human remedy for this darkness. (So she should not feel responsible for it.) Another was that "feeling" the presence of Jesus was not the only or even the primary evidence of his presence. (Jesus himself said by their fruits—not their certainty—you shall know them.) In fact, the very craving for God was a "sure sign" that God was present—though in a hidden way—in her life. And the third bit of wisdom was that the pain she was going through could be redemptive. Jesus himself had to experience the agony of the absence of God: "My God, my God, why have you forsaken me?" And as his suffering was redemptive for us, so Mother Teresa could suffer redemptively by holding on to God in the midst of the darkness.

Still, what good can God's silence do for us ... for me?

Last spring I had a memorable day. My daughter graduated from college, I turned fifty years old, and I spoke at her commencement—all on the same day. But the most memorable line of the day involved none of that. A man named David Winter had been president of her school for over a quarter of a century. Toward the end of his term, as he was looking forward to retirement, he suffered a disease that over a period of three weeks robbed him of his sight. As we processed up to the graduation platform, he had to hold the arm of another to guide him. And in his words of greeting to the students and parents, he said, "Never doubt in the darkness what God has shown you in the light."

This became Mother Teresa's last, great gift to the world.

Maybe there is a good reason why God doesn't show up in the sky with a giant Michelangeloid face for a showdown. Perhaps God's goal for the human race is more than just getting people to admit that he exists. (Author Robert Nozick notes how we often wish we could coerce people into believing things; we speak of *knockdown* arguments and *attacks* of logic. "Perhaps philosophers need arguments so powerful they set up reverberations in the brain: if the person refuses to accept the conclusion, he *dies*. How's that for a powerful argument?") *Forcing* people to admit that God exists does not really solve the core problem of the human race. Even if they admit that God exists, the problem of the human heart remains.

For example, imagine you're driving down the road and you see a black and white squad car on the street near you. You suddenly find your intention to obey the speed limit going way up. But it's not because your heart has changed. You have not suddenly found that your deep inner driving convictions have changed and you find yourself loving the existence of a speed limit. No, you're just doing pain avoidance. If the officer stops you—and don't pretend this has never happened for you—you may even, in your secret heart of hearts, nurse bad thoughts about him.

> Forcing people to admit that God exists does not really solve the core problem of the human race. Even if they admit that God exists, the problem of the human heart remains.

You may find yourself thinking, *There are murderers and thieves out there. He ought to be out there chasing bad guys now instead of picking on an honest, tax-paying citizen like me.* Or you may find yourself thinking, *He's probably just after his quota. I know those guys. They have quotas, and he's probably after his quota.* Some of you will even try to flirt with the officer to avoid getting the ticket. Someone in my own marriage—not I—has actually done such a thing.

What happens is that our own darkness and self-preoccupation prevent us from seeing the officer of the law objectively for who he is. We are projecting onto him our own fears, our own desires, our own selfishness, and our own darkness. All of those things filter the way we see that human being. This goes on all the time for us and affects all of our relationships.

Now, when it comes to seeing God, multiply this a thousand

times over, and we begin to see part of God's problem in dealing with the human race. The writers of Scripture put it like this: "No one can see God's face" (see Exodus 33:20).

What do they mean when they say that no one can see God's face? They mean that we cannot see God as he is. We are not capable of this. We inevitably project our own fallenness onto God.

So just getting people to believe in the existence of God or the existence of the supernatural does no good. People can believe in the supernatural but still have lives that are moral or spiritual disasters. James put it like this: "You believe that there is one God. Good! Even the demons believe that—and shudder" (James 2:19). Do these demons believe that the one God is good and just and fair and loving? Do these demons believe the same things about this God that Jesus believed about his Father? No. Not at all.

God seems to present himself to us in such a way that people who want to dismiss God will be able to dismiss him. He seems to leave space for them. People who do not want there to be a God will find a way to believe that there is no God. Blaise Pascal said that there is enough light for those who want to see and enough darkness for those of a different persuasion.

2. Why Not a Better Product?

Sometimes I am troubled about God's existence when I think about his constituency. If Christianity is true, why aren't Christians better advertisements? And why doesn't God speak up about that?

This objection takes a strong form. Sam Harris, who wrote *Letter to a Christian Nation* and *The End of Faith*, argues that religion actually poses the greatest threat to civilization and human survival. This has been a common theme since 9/11 and the emergence of the threat of terrorist attacks. It was believers who led the Crusades, the Inquisition, and the Salem witch trials. It was believers who used the Bible to defend slavery and who still use it to defend the subjugation of women. An atheist named Steven Weinberg puts it like this: "Good people do good things, and bad people do bad things, but to get good people to do bad things, that takes religion." Many horrible things have been done in the name of God—even in the name of the God of the Bible. It does no good to minimize these offenses or attempt to justify them. The apostle Peter himself wrote, "It is time for judgment to begin with the family of God" (1 Peter 4:17).

One question that helps settle my doubts is this: Were these horrible atrocities the outcome of Jesus' teaching or violations of it? The Jesus who said, "Love your enemies." The Jesus who said, "Bless those who persecute you." The Jesus who said, "When somebody hits you, turn the other cheek." The Jesus who said on the cross, "Father, forgive them for they know not what they do."

Another question that seems important is this: Has the human race done better in societies that seek to eliminate faith altogether?

The greatest bloodbaths in the history of the human race were recorded in the twentieth century in countries that sought to eliminate God, worship, and faith. Stalin is thought to have been responsible for twenty million deaths. Mikhail Gorbachev put that estimate at closer to thirty-five million. A recent book reported that Mao Tse-tung alone, in China, was responsible for something like seventy million deaths. Hitler, in Nazi Germany, was responsible for somewhere around ten million deaths. Pol Pot in Cambodia ran an atheist regime where it is estimated that 20 percent of the population of his entire country was massacred under his hand. Elie Wiesel, who lost his family in the Holocaust, wrote, "The programmatic absence of a God, or at least the illusion of opposing his presence, leads systematically to horror."

Sometimes I try a little thought experiment. Imagine a society with no religion, no faith, no God. (It has been attempted.) Does it seem likely that in that society no one is going to covet someone else's money, no one is going to covet someone else's house or someone else's spouse, that people whose skin tones are different suddenly are going to become one another's devoted servants? The problem of "otherness" is suddenly going to be solved? It is hard to imagine that just because religion is done away with, greedy people will become generous, angry people will become merciful, Jerry Springer will be canceled, and everyone will support PBS and listen to NPR.

> Imagine a society with no religion, no faith, no God. (It has been attempted.) Is the problem of "otherness" suddenly going to be solved?

The Crusades and the Inquisition don't produce great doubt in me, because I am more afraid of what society can become apart from faith. My doubts here come from a more mundane source. I sometimes find myself thinking I would be more certain about faith if it regularly produced a better brand of human being. Writer David Kinnaman calls his thoughtful book *Unchristian* because his research reveals that most people outside Christianity view Christians as characterized by "unchristian" people. One interviewee put it like this: "Most people I meet assume that *Christian* means very conservative, entrenched in their thinking, antigay, antichoice, angry, violent, illogical, empire builders; they want to convert everyone, and they generally cannot live peacefully with anyone who doesn't believe what they believe."

And the preachers. Don't get me started. Frederick Buechner has written, "There is perhaps no better proof for the existence of God than the way year after year he survives the way his professional friends promote him."

Of course, any believer will tell you that we would all be much worse on our own. Author Evelyn Waugh was a Catholic who fell pretty woefully short of his faith's standards. Somebody asked Waugh one time, "How can you call yourself a Catholic and be so badly behaved, so mean, such a jerk, so spiteful?"

Waugh responded, "Just imagine me if I were not a Catholic."

And I know—nonbelievers are hypocrites as well. This is the human condition. Hypocrisy is the tribute that virtue pays to vice, the old saying goes. But still ...

I have been around Christians my whole life. And personally, this objection of "unChristian Christians" troubles my faith a lot. I know there are explanations. For instance:

— Only God sees the heart.

— Jesus preferred hanging out with sinners to hanging out with saints, who were after all the ones who crucified him.

— Not everyone who calls Jesus "Lord" is really a follower.

— Alternative ideologies from Marxism to psychoanalysis haven't set the world on fire.

"That psychoanalysis has not made the analysts themselves better, nobler, or of stronger character remains a disappointment for me," Freud wrote to a friend. "Perhaps I was wrong to expect it."

But I have to say that, in my darker moods, the low percentage of Christians who really seem to be moving on the path to "new creaturehood" troubles my faith.

And the lack of progress that troubles me most is my own.

3. Why Not End the Pain?

One more question: If there really is an all-loving, all-powerful, all-good, and competent God overseeing the universe, why is there so much evil and so much suffering and so much pain? Why are there natural disasters like tsunamis and earthquakes, accidents like car crashes and fires, diseases like heart attacks and cancer and Alzheimer's and multiple sclerosis? Why don't we hear from God; why don't we get help from him in these valleys of human pain? Steve Weinberg says, "The God of birds and trees would also have to be the God of birth defects and cancer."

This question about God's silence is as old as belief in him. A philosopher named Diagoras was Greece's most famous atheist in the fifth century BC. Someone once pointed out to him a display of pictures showing the gods at work. "You think the gods have no care for man? Look at all the pictures of those who escaped storms by praying to the gods for escape." Diagoras replied, "Yes indeed, but where are the pictures of all those who suffered shipwreck and perished in the waves?"

People sometimes sidestep the issue of unanswered suffering by telling a story about how God stepped into their tragic circumstances and saved them. They have holes in their stories, though.

A friend of mine nearly drowned along with his son recently. They were sucked out by a vicious riptide at a beach that was deserted other than his family. When he realized what they were fighting against, he thought of how his family was going to face a double funeral and may not even be able to find their bodies.

His cousin saw their struggle and went in to point to where they should swim. Eventually, just barely, they made it. My friend's efforts to get to shore were so Herculean that his kidneys shut down, and he actually had to go on dialysis for a while. (And he was an Olympic decathlete, so it took a lot to wear his body down.)

A few of his friends who came to pray for him said they just knew God would restore his kidneys; they just knew God had plans of health and vitality for him. He would wonder, when he went in for dialysis, about all the other people who had been on dialysis for years. Did God have no good plans for their vitality? How did his friends know about him? And what about all of the other suffering that goes unrelieved? For believers and unbelievers?

It is striking that in some religions, evil and suffering do not constitute the basis for an intellectual problem. In Hinduism, for example, suffering is a result of bad karma left over from a previous life. If you are suffering in this life, you are working off bad choices that you made in a past life. In Buddhism, both suffering and joy are understood to be illusory—the result of human desire. The Buddha said that true enlightenment includes awareness that the self does not exist. Once you understand that you have no self, there is no reason to avoid pain. (Not having a self also comes in handy when the IRS tries to audit you.)

There is much about this question I don't understand. But one man, whose son died climbing a mountain when he was twenty-five, said that what he came to see was "tears, a weeping God, suffering over my suffering. I had not realized that if God loves the world, God suffers. I had thoughtlessly supposed God loved without suffering. I knew that divine love was the key. But I had not realized that the divine love that is the key is a suffering love."

> People sometimes sidestep the issue of unanswered suffering by telling a story about how God stepped into their tragic circumstances and saved them. Yet they have holes in their stories.

Jesus introduced us to a suffering God, something the world had never thought of before. I don't know the full answer, but I do know those things.

I'm struck not only by what might be called the "strange silence of God," but also by what might be called the "silence of atheism" or the "silence of no God." That is not a strange silence. That silence is not a puzzle, not a riddle. That silence is a silence that says, "That's all there is. Just silence." No answer. No meaning. No nothing.

Betting Your Life

We may not like the silence; we may not have chosen to have unanswered questions, but we must choose how we will understand them, what we will bet our lives on. I invite you to consider two alternatives and their consequences. One of them, to paraphrase atheist Bertrand Russell, is "You are the product of causes that have no purpose or meaning. Your origin, your growth, your hopes, fears, loves, beliefs are the outcome of accidental collections of atoms. No fire, heroism, or intensity of thought or feeling can preserve your life from beyond the grave. All the devotion, all the inspiration, all the labor of all the ages are destined to extinction in the vast death of the solar system. The whole temple of human achievement must inevitably be buried in the debris of a universe in ruins. That's what we're all headed for."

> We all have the sense, not just that life is hard, not just that we suffer. We have the sense not just that things are bad, but that things are not the way they're supposed to be.

Or you can choose this: "You are the uniquely designed creation of a thoroughly good and unspeakably creative God. You are made in his image, with a capacity to reason, choose, and love that sets you above all other life forms. You will not only survive death, but you yourself were made to bear an eternal weight of glory you cannot now even fathom and you will one day know."

You must decide which one to bet your life on.

A cartoon in the *San Francisco Chronicle* illustrates this truth wonderfully. Two atheists are going door-to-door introducing their religious beliefs. They stand in front of an open door, and the man inside says, "This pamphlet is blank." They answer, "We're atheists."

If there is no God, there is no story. There is nothing to write, no guideline, no indicator. Nothing makes any difference. Do whatever you want to do! The pamphlet is blank. The universe is silent.

The mere fact that atheism might be depressing does not mean that it is false. If it is true, we may as well own up to it now.

But we all have this sense, not just that life is hard, not just that we suffer. We have this sense not just that things are bad, but *that things are not the way they're supposed to be.* Children are not *supposed* to grow up with no one caring about them, no one providing for their education and health just because they're the wrong color. Women are not *supposed* to be abused. Dads are not *supposed* to die of cancer when they are forty years old and their children are young.

If the universe is a machine, a giant accident, a blind, pitiless indifference, *where did we get the idea that there is a way that things are supposed to be?*

This is a very simple picture. It is not philosophically profound, but it helps me to think about it in a simple way: A woman I know named Sheryl went to a salon to have her nails manicured. As the beautician began to work, they began to have a good conversation about many subjects. When they eventually touched on God, the beautician said, "I don't believe God exists."

"Why do you say that?" asked Sheryl, who has MS.

"Well, you just have to go out on the street to realize God doesn't exist. Tell me, if God exists, would there be so many sick people? Would there be abandoned children? If God existed, there would be neither suffering nor pain. I can't imagine loving a God who could allow all these things."

Sheryl thought for a moment. She didn't respond because she didn't want to start an argument. The beautician finished her job, and Sheryl left the shop.

Just after she left the beauty shop, she saw a woman in the street with long, stringy, dirty hair. She looked filthy and unkempt. Sheryl turned, entered the beauty shop again, and said to the beautician, "You know what? Beauticians do not exist."

"How can you say that?" asked the surprised beautician. "I am here. I just worked on you. I exist."

"No," Sheryl exclaimed, "beauticians do not exist, because if they did, there would be no people with dirty, long hair and appearing very unkempt like that woman outside!"

"Ah, but beauticians do exist," she answered. "The problem is, people do not come to me."

Exactly.

The main problem with doubt, when doubt gets toxic, is not what it does to us. It is what it keeps us from doing.

WHEN DOUBT
GOES BAD

Life is just a dirty trick
from nothingness to nothingness.
ERNEST HEMINGWAY

If you were to ask me who largely shaped my faith during my most formative years, the answer would be easy. He was a middle-aged professor of Greek in my college named Jerry Hawthorne. He had a big shock of red hair, so we called him *Megas Rodos*, Greek for Big Red.

Learning koine Greek at eight o'clock in the morning might seem tedious to some. But it was a highlight life experience for the circle of guys I hung out with: Chuck, a premed student who became my first and best friend when we were fifteen years old; Kevin, whom we hung around with because he was funny and charming and because we hoped to pick up the girls he discarded; Tommy, who could make a stone laugh; and the Ox, a prelaw student who had a gift for falling asleep in class without being noticed and still getting A's. We used to say that Ox would one day try cases and sum up: "Your honor, the defense rests. *Zzzzz ...*"

Over time we became not just Megas Rodos's students, but his friends. We would have donuts together on Wednesday mornings when there was no required chapel (chapel attendance on other days was monitored by students fondly known as "chapel spies") and on other mornings when we were using up our skip days. On Friday afternoons we would meet in the student union. Someone would prepare a paper (not for a class, just for the joy of learning), and we would all discuss it. Big Red would invite us to his home. He followed our careers, officiated at our weddings, guided us to graduate school, and warned our girlfriends and later our wives about us.

He was the worst joke teller I have ever known. He would spoil the punch line long before getting there, interrupt himself repeatedly, turn bright red in anticipation of how funny it was going to be, then jab mercilessly with a bony elbow at whoever was sitting next to him to elicit more laughter. He would recite Monty Python routines in a horribly inept falsetto British accent. His favorite involved a British middle-aged housewife proving to another woman that she knew the French existentialist Jean-Paul Sartre by calling up Sartre's home long distance and getting Mrs. Sartre:

"Hallooo. Is this the home of Jean-Paul Sartre?"
(Mrs. Sartre) "Yes."
"Is Jean-Paul free?"
(Mrs. Sartre) "That's what he's been trying to figure out for thirty years, dearie! Ha, ha, ha, ha ..."

We all adored him. There was something about his character, something about the way he took both his subject matter and his students so seriously, something about his earthy sense of humor and his deep humility before God that made everyone around him want to be a better person. He introduced us to great scholars and great books. He was the kind of person who — by sheer dint of character — made you ashamed of giving less than your best effort.

Once two of us snuck into his office and stole some of his stationery. We wrote a note to one his students who had missed a number of classes. The note, in our best Hawthornian style, was an apology for not having taught better, for letting this student down. Then we stood outside his office when the student came bursting in: "Oh no, Dr. Hawthorne, you didn't let me down. I let you down! But I'm not missing any more classes!" Poor Big Red, of course, had no idea what prompted this meltdown.

For years now whenever I have met people who graduated from my college I have asked them who most influenced them. One name is repeated over and over. There is no close second.

Big Red opened up a world of questions I had never encountered in my Baptist church growing up. Every question led to more questions, but they also led to more faith. Maybe if God could use real people to write Scripture, maybe if Jesus really did come as a man rather than a superhero with his cape hidden behind his back, maybe life with God is more possible for someone like me than I had dared to think. To be able to think and poke and doubt and ask made faith a living, breathing thing to me. You can plant the mustard seed of faith in a Styrofoam cup of dirt to start, but eventually it must go into the broad earth where it has space to spread out; it will die of too much confinement. This is perhaps an odd way to say it, but Big Red taught me how doubt could make me a better believer.

A student who went to Wheaton a few years ahead of me had transferred in from Moody Bible Institute (where, as the saying went, "Bible is our middle name"). He was warned that Wheaton was on the liberal side. He, too, became a student of Jerry Hawthorne. He, too, had his mind opened by the questions and study.

But in this student's case, the questions led to his faith crumbling. His name is Bart Ehrman, and he tells his story in his *New York Times* bestselling book, *Misquoting Jesus*, so I am not revealing anything new. He tells how Jerry influenced his life as a scholar, teacher, and eventually friend. He speaks of how he was struck by Jerry's not being afraid of asking questions of his faith—a tendency that struck Bart as a weakness.

Eventually Bart began to ask questions as well. But the notion that the Bible had a human side seemed to him proof that it could not be divine. The only alternative to simpleminded fundamentalism to him seemed to be to reject God altogether. The same teacher and the same questions that deepened my faith dismantled his. For a time he described himself as a "cheerful agnostic"; more recently he categorized himself as an atheist. He now chairs the department of religious studies at the University of North Carolina at Chapel Hill, which seems to me an odd occupation for a man who does not believe in God, but I know he has thought long and hard and painfully over important questions and wants to point to the truth.

> He and I admired the same teacher, were disturbed and excited by the same questions, and were exposed to the same learning. Yet those experiences led to the growth of faith in one and the growth of doubt in the other.

Bart and I went to the same school, admired the same teacher, were disturbed and excited by the same questions, and were exposed to the same learning. Yet those experiences led to the growth of faith in one and the growth of doubt in the other. I don't know why.

Sometimes doubt can do good in us. It can motivate us to study and learn. It can purify false beliefs that have crept into our faith. It can humble our arrogance. It can give us patience and compassion with other doubters. It can remind us of how much truth matters. Martin Luther, who was the champion of the importance of faith but wrestled with doubt himself, insisted that pride—not doubt—is the opposite of faith.

But doubt can go bad; doubt can curdle like spoiled milk. Doubt can seep from the mind into the will and block courage and devotion. It can damage our capacity to persevere. It can make us indecisive. It can erode confidence. The Solidarity movement in Poland had a memorable slogan: "Pessimism of the mind, optimism of the will." They understood that they faced uncertainty about their outcome, but they refused to allow the uncertainty of their success to weaken the strength of their devotion.

Therapists sometimes speak of "secondary gain" when they analyze problems. For instance, a young boy may suffer from psychosomatic illness. A shrewd therapist notes all the ways he benefits from being sick: he gets to stay home from school, he gets loving TLC from his mom, he gets to skip homework and watch TV, he becomes the center of attention. His illness feels real to him, but it is not caused purely by germs. If we're honest about it, our doubts can produce secondary gains as well. So let's look at some of the ways doubting goes bad and the "secondary gain" behind it.

The Skeptic

The skeptic is someone who says, "I'm going to suspend judgment. I'm not going to commit myself, because the demand for sufficient evidence has not yet been met." This reasoning may sound objective or rational, but the dynamic that is going on underneath the surface in the skeptic is this: "I don't want to be wrong. I don't want to be hurt. I don't want to look like I'm one of the gullible ones." Underneath the surface of the skeptic is fear — fear of being disappointed. The skeptic says, "I would rather stand on the sidelines and look like an intelligent observer than risk trusting. I will forgo all that might come with that trust."

My favorite story about a skeptic takes place back in the time of the French Revolution, during the "Reign of Terror." People were being executed right and left. Three men were waiting to be executed. The first one was a priest. As he was brought to the guillotine, he was asked, "Do you have any last words?" He answered,

"I believe God is going to save me." He put his head into place, the blade came down, and it stopped two inches from his neck. The executioners said, "This is a miracle," and they let him go.

The next man came up. He, too, was a priest. The executioners asked him, "Do you have any last words?" "I believe God is going to save me," he said. They put him in the block, the blade came down, and it stopped two inches from his neck. They said, "This is a miracle," and they let him go.

The third man came up. He was a skeptic and an atheist. He did not want to be associated with believers. The executioners asked him, "Do you have any last words?" Looking at the guillotine, he said, "Well, I think I see your problem. There's something jammed in the gear mechanism."

Skeptics would rather, even at their own expense, appear to be right than take the risk of trusting.

One of the disciples was so well known for this kind of skepticism that it earned him a nickname: "Doubting Thomas." We see him three times in the gospel of John, and he is always expressing skepticism.

One aspect of doubt gone bad that Thomas illustrates is how it robs us of confidence and hope. Jesus was going to Bethany to help Mary and Martha. Lazarus was ill and in fact was going to die. The disciples tried to dissuade Jesus from going, because Jesus was in hot water back there. Jesus, however, would not be dissuaded. "Then Thomas (called Didymus) said to the rest of the disciples, 'Let us also go, that we may die with him'" (John 11:16).

This is not the kind of comment that fires up a team with anticipation and energy. One of the metaphors writer William Sessions uses to describe faith involves the horizon. The horizon is the farthest point of our vision. It is the place of possibility, the place to which we are always called. Faith is, among other things, embracing our horizon. When doubt goes bad, we become afraid. Horizon gets challenged.

But the depth of Thomas's doubt occurred after Jesus appeared to the other disciples who were gathered together after the resurrection. All of them were there except Thomas. They were overjoyed and couldn't wait to tell Thomas. It is interesting that the text doesn't say why Thomas wasn't with them. Was he distancing himself from them? We don't know. But they couldn't wait to tell him. "Thomas, we saw him! He is alive! He is risen from the dead!" They were stunned by Thomas's response: "I don't believe you."

What Thomas was saying to the other disciples was that they were either lying or delusional. He knew better. He knew them. He knew Jesus. He had heard him teach and seen him perform miracles. More than any other human being, Thomas had good reasons to believe. But he chose the skeptic path, and he gave a striking response: "Unless I see the nail marks in his hands and put my finger where the nails were, and put my hand into his side, I will not believe it" (John 20:25).

The phrase "doubting Thomas" never occurs in the Bible, but there he has another nickname that sheds light on doubt gone wrong. Twice John mentions that he is Thomas, also called Didymus, the Greek word for "twin." Names have significance in ancient writings, and John surely doesn't mention this one twice by accident. Nowadays twins are often celebrated, but twins in the ancient world were generally regarded as negative omens. They messed up laws of inheritance. The mortality rate around twin births was much higher than single births.

> *Skeptics would rather, even at their own expense, appear to be right than take the risk of trusting.*

There is another way in which Thomas's name is significant. In many languages, including ancient Greek, there is a connection between the words for "doubt" and "two." We have a similar case in English in the relationship between "doubt" and "double."

To doubt is to be of two minds. The Chinese speak memorably of a person "having a foot in two boats." In Guatemala the Kekchi language speaks of a person "whose heart is made two."

When doubt takes this form, it creates what James calls "double-mindedness" (see James 1:5–8). A double-minded person, he says, is unstable, like a wave on the sea driven forward one moment and backward the next. This person is torn in two directions at once. He wants to be generous, but he wants to hoard stuff for himself. He wants to be humble, but he wants to make sure everybody notices and applauds him for it. This doubt creates a kind of spiritual double bind. (Here is my favorite true story about a spiritual double bind. My friend Gary had an uncle who was a Pentecostal faith healer. At one service he spoke directly to the demon he was seeking to exorcise from a man who had come forward: "What's your name, demon?" The demon indicated he was "the spirit of lying." Gary's uncle demanded: "Are you telling me the truth, lying demon?")

> Skepticism can keep us from blessing, can keep us trapped in two minds. But there are other forms of doubt that are more dangerous than skepticism.

The double-mindedness of Thomas's doubt is what was most destructive. But it was not fatal. Thomas really did want to know. If the negative side of skepticism is doubt, the positive side is the hope that a hidden reality may yet reveal itself. It is this hoping side of skepticism that led Blaise Pascal to write, "There has never been a real complete skeptic." Jesus came to Thomas as he often does for skeptical folks, and Thomas believed. Jesus said, "Because you have seen me, you have believed; blessed are those who have not seen and yet have believed" (John 20:29). This statement is sometimes mistakenly taken as endorsing irrational faith. But that is not Jesus' point. There are many things we cannot "see" — from electricity to love and justice — that are a blessing to believe. Skepticism can keep us from blessing, can keep us trapped in two minds. But there are other forms of doubt that are more dangerous than skepticism.

The Cynic

The second way that doubt goes bad is cynicism. Unlike skeptics, people driven by cynicism are not so much looking for answers as they are offering conclusions. They offer conclusions about the world that paint it in an entirely negative light: The world is not fair. People can't be trusted. Circumstances typically get worse. Bad things always happen to good people. Good things only happen to other people. God is simply a matter of wishful thinking, so we might as well not think about him at all.

Give a skeptic a hug, and she will doubt that you really mean it. Give a cynic a hug, and he will check for his wallet to see if you've picked his pocket.

Scratch the surface of any cynic, and you will find a wounded idealist underneath. Because of previous pain or disappointment, cynics make their conclusions about life before the questions have even been asked. This means that beyond just seeing what is wrong with the world, cynics lack the courage to do something about it. The dynamic beneath cynicism is a fear of accepting responsibility.

A skeptic is afraid of getting taken in. A cynic is afraid of having to measure up. Skeptics abstain from voting. Cynics abstain too, then write columns criticizing all the candidates.

A biblical example of this is a man named Pontius Pilate. In Jesus' day, Pontius Pilate was the highest-ranking official in Judea. He was educated and powerful, and he possessed great authority. He had to keep the Romans off his back and the Jews out of his face. Maybe when he was younger he had believed in law and justice, but he had been around power a long time. Anybody who might call on him to believe in something enough to have to sacrifice for it was a troublemaker.

When Jesus, a simple carpenter, was brought before Pilate and claimed he could testify to the truth, Pilate responded by asking, "What is truth?" (John 18:38). What he was really saying was: "How can you truly be certain of anything? What kind of knowledge do you think you have? What kind of difference do you really think you can make? Why don't you just stop trying to save the world, and all this trouble will go away?" The encounter brings to mind Edward Gibbon's observation on what happened to faith in the decline of Rome: "Toward the end of the Roman Empire, all religions were regarded by the people as equally true, by the philosophers as equally false, and by the politicians as equally useful."

Gullible masses, skeptical intellectuals, cynical power brokers.

> The danger of cynicism is that this isn't an answer. It's no answer at all. It's just a way to avoid the question. Cynicism is the opposite of a trumpet call; it is the call to inaction.

Pilate was not so much seeking answers as he was trying to avoid responsibility. As Matthew writes in his gospel: "When Pilate saw that he was getting nowhere, but that instead an uproar was starting, he took water and washed his hands in front of the crowd. 'I am innocent of this man's blood,' he said. 'It is your responsibility!'" (27:24). In essence Pilate was saying, "I'm washing my hands of this. This is now someone else's problem." As a person in the twenty-first century might say, "Whatever. Whatever."

I have tried to wash my hands of a lot of stuff in my life to avoid responsibility for it. In case something doesn't go well at work, I have decided that it will be somebody else's fault. I have washed my hands of it. In case something goes wrong with this book, it will be my editor's fault.

When facing a difficult decision, a moral responsibility, or a potentially unpopular choice, cynics choose to wash their hands and conclude, "Whatever." Or worse, when facing some of life's most difficult questions (Does God exist? If he does, does he have my best interest in mind? If he does, does he call me to live in a certain way?), if there is even a shred of doubt, cynics choose to wash their hands. What is truth anyway? The danger of cynicism is that this isn't an answer. It's no answer at all. It's just a way to avoid the question. Cynicism is the opposite of a trumpet call; it is the call to inaction.

The word *cynic* comes from the Greek word for dog. The original cynics were followers of the ancient philosopher Diogenes and were called dogs because they proposed to live like dogs—no conventions, no shame. They believed the universe had no meaning and that all human aspirations were mere pretension. "Diogenes' advice is that we stop distracting ourselves with accomplishments, accept the meaninglessness of the universe, lie down on a park bench and get some sun while we have the chance."

Oddly enough, churches—houses of faith—can be breeding grounds for cynicism. When leaders use spiritual language to cover up their drive for power, control, and applause, cynicism springs up like dandelions. Not just doubt, but the wrong kind of faith leads to cynicism as well. I have a friend who used to work on staff at a church. He writes books about the truth of Christianity. He speaks at churches sometimes. But he is not a part of one himself. He got tired and burnt out by the constant promotion and hype and pressure to be bigger. He and his wife have some friends over on Sunday mornings sometimes. They are mostly longtime Christians who have gotten cynical about churches. Most of them used to be staff members. The dirty little and poorly kept secret of many churches is that the most cynical people in them are often on the payroll.

The Rebel

But there is an even more destructive way that doubt can hurt us. The third category of mismanaged doubt doesn't go simply by one name. It is sometimes called "unbelief" in the Bible, but it is very different than uncertainty. This is the severest form of doubt gone wrong. Unbelief is refusal to trust. It is not uncertainty in the intellect; it is a settled decision of the will.

The rebel is not simply someone who *doesn't* believe. He or she is someone who doesn't *want* to believe. Rebels do not want the story of Jesus to be true. They do not want to live in the universe governed by the kind of Father whom Jesus himself trusted and described. And this desire goes so deep that it colors the way they look at every argument and every bit of evidence and makes sure they find a way not to believe.

Rebels are afraid of what would happen if they were to surrender themselves to God. So they just defy. Skeptics abstain because they don't know who to vote for. Cynics abstain because they are suspicious of everybody. Rebels don't just abstain; they secede to set up their own little dictatorship. Skeptics question, cynics suspect, rebels defy.

Edward Ruffin was a rebel of the Confederacy. He fired the first shot of the Civil War at Fort Sumter then fought the Yankees for four years. He lost his plantation and fortune along the way. When the war was over, the South had lost, and the slaves were free, he wrote a note on June 17, 1865, declaring his "unmitigated hatred to Yankee rule ... and for the perfidious, malignant, and vile Yankee race." Then he blew out his brains.

C. S. Lewis said that when he was an unbeliever, atheism was not only his *belief*, it was his strongest *desire*. "No word in my vocabulary expressed deeper hatred than the word *interference*." And he was uncomfortably aware that the Hebrew and Christian Scriptures "placed at the center what seemed to be a transcendental Interferer." Atheism appealed to his deep desire to be left along. Rebels fear being interfered with.

Sometimes the existence of God would turn out to be — borrowing a phrase from former U.S. Vice President Al Gore — "an inconvenient truth." I liked Denny, but I couldn't figure out why he kept wanting to meet. He was a large man, a construction guy, and I was a little intimidated. He wanted to talk about God, so we did, and he asked one difficult question after another about faith—one tough intellectual issue after another.

We would talk each one through to as much resolution as we could get, and he would always bring up another one. Finally, I asked him, "If all of these issues were settled, if every intellectual barrier you raised were dismantled, is there anything else besides all this intellectual stuff that would hold you back from following Jesus?"

> *He didn't want to change. His mind caused him to find all kinds of objections, but the reality was that he did not want it to be true. He was afraid of what he would have to do if it were.*

There was a long silence. Denny did not like the question. It turned out that he was involved in sexual behavior that he knew was not honoring to God and that, if he were to become a follower of Jesus, would have to change. He didn't want to change. His mind caused him to find all kinds of objections, but the reality was that he did not want it to be true. He was afraid of what he would have to do if it were.

If Denny had been smaller, I probably would have pointed this out earlier.

Saul was chosen by God to lead Israel. He was gifted, strong, and charismatic. But he had a pattern of behavior in his life that revealed he would not trust God enough to obey him. This went on for such a long time that, finally, God could not use him anymore and chose David to be the new king.

Initially Saul had liked David, but when he discovered that David was to replace him on Israel's throne, he would not surrender to God, would not surrender his crown, would not obey God. Finally, he ended up turning to the occult. He went to visit a woman known as the witch of Endor to ask her to conjure up the spirit of Samuel the prophet, an occult practice that would have been an abomination to him when he was a young man. As G. K. Chesterton wrote, if people cease to believe in God, they do not believe in nothing but in anything. In the end, Saul took his own life in despair rather than bend his knee before God. This is rebellion toward God. This is unbelief.

What Do We *Want*?

"What do I *want* to believe?" is one of the most important questions we can ask when it comes to the search for faith.

It is crucial to be honest about this, because over time we have a tendency to find ourselves believing what we *want* to believe. Remember, Bart called himself a "cheerful" agnostic. Philosopher Thomas Nagel wrote, "I want atheism to be true. It isn't just that I don't believe in God. I don't want there to be a God. I don't want the universe to be like that."

Maybe Marx was right—faith is the opium of the people, exploited by the elite to stay in power. Maybe some people have a "god gene" that predisposes them to believe just as others are genetically predisposed to become alcoholics or left-handers or yodelers. Maybe Freud was right and "the religions of mankind must be classed among the mass delusions ... the universal obsessional neurosis of humanity." Freud proposed in *Totem and Taboo* that both religious faith and guilt arose when a primal horde of men grew jealous of their father—a despot who had seized all the women for himself—and therefore killed him, ate his body, and then instituted the ritual sacrifice of an animal ("totem") as a way to displace their guilt. Belief in God is just a giant oedipal projection of our wishes upon the cosmos. Freud actually seriously argued that religion started because an early tribe of men killed the father and felt guilty about it and invented religion to deal with their guilt and make sure it wouldn't get repeated. This particular idea of his has not caught on widely.

Karl Marx's drug analogy can cut both ways. Nobel laureate Czeslaw Milosz observed in *The Discreet Charm of Nihilism*, "A true opium of the people is the belief of nothingness after death — a huge solace for thinking that we are not going to be judged for our betrayals, greed, cowardice, murders."

The reason this question is important for us is that if we *want* to, we can find ways that explain away every reason for faith: the existence of creation; stories of answered prayer; evidence of the resurrection; testimonies of changed lives; the unmatched wisdom of Jesus; and the tugging and longing of your own heart for grace, forgiveness, meaning, wholeness, transcendence, and heaven. If you want badly enough not to believe, you will find a way not to believe.

I often find myself wishing, given the damage that doubt can do, that God would just remove it. But he generally doesn't. Maybe he has a reason not to.

9

THE GIFT
OF UNCERTAINTY

*Almost nothing that makes any real
difference can be proved.*

FREDERICK BUECHNER

I met my wife on a blind date. We were set up by a married couple named Greg and Bonnie, and neither of us was too excited about a blind date to begin with (even the name is ominous). We ended up talking in the backyard of the place where I lived, in a lovely nook overlooking the Arroyo Valley with the Rose Bowl situated far below. After a time Nancy became noticeably quiet. I looked over and saw that she had fallen asleep. So the date didn't really seem as if it was going all that well by my standards. And my standards were not high. A flight on the *Hindenburg* would have been more fun than a date with me on one of my off nights.

On the other hand, maybe Nancy just felt comfortable around me. So I thought I'd give it another shot. My problem was that I did not know how to get in touch with her. Greg and Bonnie had returned to their home in the Midwest, and I had no phone numbers for anybody. All I knew about Nancy was that she attended a church in my denomination in Whittier, California. So I called the church receptionist. "My name is John Ortberg," I explained. "I need the phone number of one of your parishioners, a young woman named Nancy Berg. I work as a pastor at First Baptist Church at La Crescenta. It's kind of a ministry thing."

There was a long pause. The receptionist put me on hold for a good five minutes. What I did not know then, and what no one told me for another six months, was that the receptionist at the church was Nancy's mother, Verna Berg. And she put me on hold so she could call her daughter and ask if she wanted her phone number given out. On such a slender thread did the future existence of our children hang.

> *Many people, when they consider faith, think,* I believe that God exists *or* Love is the greatest virtue. *But at its core, faith is not simply the belief in a statement; it puts trust in a person.*

Sometimes, as we dated, Nancy was less certain about me. We dated only a few times before she left for grad school a few thousand miles away, and when I didn't write as often as she had hoped for, she figured I was not too interested. Then I found out she was dating another guy, and I knew I was interested. (I have a little Maurice Chevalier in me.) I called her long distance. I stumbled around awhile. "I guess what I'm trying to say," I said, "is I like you." Silence. I figured maybe she'd fallen asleep again.

And so it went. In fact, the hardest part of our relationship was uncertainty. I did not expect or want it. I had never had a serious relationship before, and I thought a person was supposed to "just know." I did not understand that it is the uncertainty that demands that you to get to know yourself really well — what you value, what you want — by questioning, choosing, risking, and committing.

Dating, like faith, is an exercise in strategic uncertainty. André Comte-Sponville notes that it is precisely the experience of uncertainty that makes possible the euphoria of what we call falling in love. We go through intense questioning, wondering, hoping, and doubting. *Does she really care?* And when that is followed by evidence that she *does* care, we have an endorphin tidal wave. It is precisely this roller-coaster ride of the agony of uncertainty and the ecstasy of relief that gives the early stages of love their emotional TNT. It is also why, as love matures, as commitment becomes sure, the roller coaster must inevitably settle down.

Faith is not simply holding beliefs. Many people, when they consider faith, think, *I believe that God exists*, or *Scripture is accurate*, or *Love is the greatest virtue*. But at its core, faith is not simply the belief in a statement; it *puts trust in a person*.

We all think we want certainty. But we don't. What we really want is trust, wisely placed. Trust is better than certainty because it honors the freedom of persons and makes possible growth and intimacy that certainty alone could never produce.

There can be no intimacy without trust. Let's say someone asks me, "John, is your wife faithful to you?" I say, "Yes." He asks, "But how do you know?" I answer, "I know my wife." He says, "But she could be fooling you. Wouldn't you like to know? Let's remove all uncertainty. Let's say we could create a 'Nancy cam,' and keep her under surveillance twenty-four hours a day. Wouldn't you want that?"

A friend of ours is a brilliant engineer. He testifies before Congress on tech issues. He understands our TiVo. He has a young daughter and in their house they have cameras that can be on her all the time. We joke that as she grows up, he will have a "daughter cam" on that girl twenty-four hours a day. I wouldn't want to be his daughter. More than that, I wouldn't want to date his daughter. And I wouldn't want a "Nancy cam" even if I could have one. I wouldn't want to know. I would rather trust, because when you trust someone, you give him or her a gift, and you enter into a kind of dance. When I trust, I take a risk. I choose to be vulnerable. When my wife in turn is faithful, we reach a deeper level of intimacy. There is no other way to intimacy and depth of relationship between persons than to trust.

In a world of objects and machines, this is not so. In that world we try to remove all uncertainty. We want to be able to predict. We want control. The world of persons is another world. When it comes to persons, trusting is better than predicting and controlling.

Have you ever seen the movie *The Stepford Wives*? The wives in Stepford are systematically replaced by robots that look exactly like them. The husbands can count on precisely the behavior they want from their cyber-spouses. No uncertainty. No frustration. No need for trust.

But, if you are a man, would you really want a woman who always dressed up for you, always fixed the food you wanted, always cleaned up after you, always agreed with whatever you said, always devoted herself to your pleasure with no will of her own? (The correct response here would be "No.")

"Stepford" is a nightmare community. Why? Because trust is the only way that loving persons relate. It can never be removed from the equation. It is the only way to honor the freedom, the dominion, and the dignity of a person. That's the way the dance works: trust, risk, vulnerability, faithfulness, intimacy.

What do you do when you trust somebody? You take a risk. It could be small, or it could be big. I go to a restaurant that you recommend. I read a book because you tell me that it is good. I tell you a secret, and then I see if you keep it confidential. I ask you to be my friend. Are you going to betray me? I invite you to be a partner in a business deal. Are you going to burn me?

Trust is something that happens between people. Trust is what holds the world of personal relationships together. This is reflected in our language all the time: *Escrow* refers to property that is held *in trust*. Universities or organizations have *boards of trustees*, people to whom the well-being of the community is *entrusted*. If you're a parent, you may put money for your children in a *trust fund*. Then your children trust that you will die on time so that they can get your money.

When I trust you, I take a little piece of myself—my stuff, my money, my time, my heart—and put it in your hands. And then I'm vulnerable. Then you respond, and I find out whether you are trustworthy and dependable. I give you the gift of my trust, and you give me the gift of your faithfulness.

That is the gift of uncertainty.

Room for Doubt Makes Trusting Possible

As long as you have faith, you will have doubts. I sometimes use the following illustration when I'm speaking. I tell the audience that I have a twenty-dollar bill in my hand and ask for a volunteer who believes me. Usually only a few hands go up. Then I tell the volunteer that I am about to destroy his (or her) faith. I open my hand and show the twenty-dollar bill. The reason I can say I am destroying his faith is that now he knows I hold the bill. He sees the bill and doesn't need faith anymore. Faith is required only when we have doubts, when we do not know for sure. When knowledge comes, faith is no more.

> Faith is required only when we have doubts, when we do not know for sure. When knowledge comes, faith is no more.

Sometimes a person is tempted to think, *I can't become a Christian because I still have doubts. I'm still not sure.* But as long as doubts exist, as long as the person is still uncertain, that is the only time faith is needed. When the doubts are gone, the person doesn't need faith anymore. Knowledge has come.

I tell the audience that this is exactly the point Paul was making in his first letter to the church at Corinth: "Now we see [that is a 'knowing' word] but a poor reflection [now we have confusion, misunderstanding, doubts, and questions] ... then we shall see face to face [we don't see face-to-face yet]. Now I know in part [with questions and doubts]; then I shall know fully, even as I am fully known" (13:12).

After talking about all this, I say that faith should be rewarded. I give the twenty-dollar bill to the volunteer. Then I ask the crowd who believes I have a thousand-dollar bill in my hand. Now many arms will shoot up. But it's too late. Sometimes people are not to be trusted. Trust by itself is neither good nor bad. It needs to be warranted.

This is part of what it means to say that faith is a *gift*. Just as beauty tends to elicit admiration, so faithfulness tends to elicit trust. As I get to know you, I find myself trusting you. But it doesn't feel to me as if the trust is something I am creating by willpower. It simply grows out of knowing that you are trustworthy. It comes as a gift.

The writer of Hebrews says, "Without faith it is impossible to please God" (11:6). That troubles folks sometimes. They wonder why we have to have faith. It's true that without faith it is impossible to please God. But without faith, it is impossible to please anybody. Try making a friend without having faith. Try getting married without faith. Try raising a child without learning about trust.

George MacDonald wrote a book called *Thomas Wingfold, Curate*, about a pastor who comes to realize he does not know whether he believes in anything spiritual. The book tells of his journey toward God. Toward the end of the book, Wingfold befriends a young man who suffers from a terminal illness. He both cares for the sick man and speaks of his own doubts.

In their final conversation, the young man asks Wingfold about his faith in God: "Are you any surer about him, sir, than you used to be?"

"At least I hope in him far more."

"Is that enough?"

"No, I want more."

The young man tells Wingfold he wishes he could come back from beyond the grave so he could let Wingfold know for sure that God exists.

Wingfold responds that even if such a thing were possible, he would not wish for it. He does not want to know for sure one minute before God wants him to know. He says he would prefer to obtain "the good of not knowing."

Knowledge is power, and uncertainty is unpleasant, so how can not knowing be good?

Uncertainty Adds Humility to Faith

"Uncertainty" is a wonderful reminder of that nagging little detail I often forget, which is that I am not God. Somebody gave me a comic strip in which St. Peter is interviewing a new arrival at the pearly gates. Peter says, "You were a believer, yes. But you skipped the not-being-a-jerk-about-it part." Not many of us have the character to handle the absolute certainty that we are right and everyone who disagrees with us is wrong. Uncertainty is one of the forms of suffering that can produce character. Maybe part of trusting God is trusting that he will give me full knowledge of him when the time is right.

> *Uncertainty is one of the forms of suffering that can produce character. Maybe part of trusting God is trusting that he will give me full knowledge of him when the time is right.*

In faith, as in dating, overconfidence can be a problem. It may sound strange, but some people would be better believers if they had a little more doubt. I know a man who went prematurely bald. (Is there any other way to go bald?) He is a big faith guy. He maintains that if he is just certain enough of an answer, God is obligated to give him what he is certain of. He is convinced that his continuing baldness is evidence of his lack of faith. He sincerely believes that if he just had enough faith, he would believe God for hair, and he would have hair. (Maybe he's right—but then, why did God create Rogaine?)

Sometimes people throw around "I have a word from the Lord" language a little loosely. Their certainty that they know everything there is to know about God keeps them from knowing the truth about themselves. "I distrust those people who know so well what God wants them to do," said suffragist Susan B. Anthony, "because I notice it always coincides with their own desires." Sometimes a little modest uncertainty would keep them from making God sound silly. My Pentecostal friend Gary was at a service once where a man stood up and addressed the congregation: "Thus saith the Lord, 'As I was with Abraham when he led the children of Israel across the desert, so shall I be with you.'" He sat down, and his wife whispered something in his ear. Then he stood back up. "Thus saith the Lord, 'I was wrong. It was Moses.'"

Job is a book of white-hot doubt. And Job is the main doubter. He doubts God's character ("know that God has wronged me and drawn his net around me," 19:6). He doubts God's goodness ("The arrows of the Almighty are in me,... my spirit drinks in their poison," 6:4). Long before Nietzsche, he charges God with absence and silence ("I cry out to you, O God, but you do not answer," 30:20). Job's friends are certain of God's presence and God's ways. Their faith is muscular. They try to speak on behalf of God to Job, to cure his doubt.

Yet when God speaks, he is on Job's side. He is angry with Job's friends "because you have not spoken of me what is right, as my servant Job has" (42:7). Somehow there was more faith in Job's honest confusion and doubting than there was in his friends' pious certainty.

Religious fanatics always lack the humility of uncertainty. The fictional Irish Mr. Dooley defined a fanatic as "a man that does what he thinks th' Lord would do if He knew th' facts of th' case."

Uncertainty Causes Us to Learn

Always our picture of God is imperfect and flawed, and doubts keep us chipping away at the truth. For instance, we tend to make God over in our own image.

One of the early doubters of the Greek Olympian gods, Greek poet Xenophanes (around 500 BCE), noted that people tended to make God look like themselves—Ethiopian gods looked Ethiopian, Thracian gods had blue eyes and red hair, all gods of the Persians looked like Persians. "If oxen and horses and lions could paint, they would all paint the gods in their own image," he wrote.

Race car driver Ricky Bobby, in the comedy *Talladega Nights*, prays, "Tiny baby infant Jesus, in your little tiny baby Jesus manger, with your little Baby Einstein developmental videos, use your little baby Jesus superpowers to help me win."

When Ricky Bobby's wife says he's supposed to pray to grown-up Jesus, he says, "No, I like the Christmas Jesus. The baby Jesus makes me feel good. So you can pray to teenage Jesus or bearded Jesus, but I'll pray to baby Jesus." We need doubt to help us know where we are making God up as we go along. "Doubts," writes Frederick Buechner, "are ants in the pants of faith; they keep it awake and moving."

Doubts also prompt us to look inside ourselves. It is not just evidence or arguments that cause doubt. Perhaps most often it is quite different. I believe that going to the dentist is good for my mouth, but when it comes time to actually go, my fear of pain causes a surge of doubtful thoughts in my mind: Is this really necessary? Is my dentist competent? Doesn't he seem a bit sadistic?

Our minds are tricky little devils. They are not just logic machines. For instance, say I have an argument with my wife over who was supposed to take the key to our hotel room. In the heat of the argument, I find all sorts of thoughts going through my mind. This is confirmation of her worst character defects. I see now what an unreasonable and judgmental person she really is. The severity of her personality flaws are revealed in high definition. Then we make up. And the thoughts that now run through my mind when I think of her produce gratitude and admiration. And she is still precisely the same person.

> Sometimes doubts are produced by philosophical arguments and questions about evidence. But far more often they come from random thoughts or moments of dryness or I-don't-even-know-what.

Doubts about God are very much that way. Sometimes they are produced by philosophical arguments and questions about evidence. Sometimes. But far more often they are produced by random thoughts or moments of dryness or I-don't-even-know-what.

Mood swings can cause doubt. I find it easier to believe in God on sunny days. When it's summertime — the living is easy, fish are jumping, cotton is high, Daddy's rich, and Mama's good-looking — I trust God is in his heaven. Three weeks of February in Chicago, and it ain't necessarily so.

Temptation causes doubt. Or maybe a better way to put it is: temptation *requires* doubt. An old adage holds that there are no atheists in foxholes. A corollary might be that there are not a whole lot of theists in brothels. Or maybe that we become adept at excluding God from our minds when he would inconvenience us. Dostoyevsky said, "If there is no God, everything is permitted." I know many atheists would disagree with this.

One thing is certain: if there is a God, then many things are not permitted. And if I want to do one of those things, my mind has to find a way to get rid of God, at least for a while. We all are at least temporary atheists, strategic atheists.

Sometimes doubt comes as mysteriously as faith. I talked to a man who said his mother always knew that God was with her. She knew that when she prayed God heard, just as a person who sticks his finger in the water knows it will get wet. He always thought this kind of faith would come to him—that he would "just know." It did not, so for a long time he discarded the whole idea of God. But he was no good at backsliding, so eventually he decided he would just accept an uncertain faith. His mother is an old woman now, with a terminal disease, and what has surprised them both is how scared she is. Now, at the end, after so many decades of blessed assurance, she doesn't know anymore.

Sometimes doubt is at work inside us, against our wishes, without our knowing. Joan Didion wrote a searingly beautiful reflection on life and death after the passing of her husband. After his sudden death, she was reflecting on the Apostles' Creed, which she had recited since childhood, when she realized she could no longer say, "I believe in the resurrection of the body." She had not chosen to stop believing it, but doubt was like a sinkhole that had been eroding the ground of faith silently, out of sight, year after year, until the power to believe was simply gone.

Uncertainty is a little prod that I need to examine not just evidence and arguments, but also my heart.

Uncertainty Pushes Us to Seek Truth

Uncertainty is a gift because it gnaws at us to pursue truth. As hunger prompts our stomach to find food, doubts prompt our minds to find reality.

Sometimes people deal with doubts by trying to repress

them—stuff them way down. I was talking with a friend recently who said, "I never read books like the one written by the atheist Richard Dawkins, because I'm afraid if I read it, it would undermine my faith." I'm not saying that you should or that you need to read every book like that one. You may not have that need, but if you don't read it and avoid it because you are afraid it will destroy your faith, then what you are really saying is, "Deep down inside, I don't believe that Jesus was really right."

When I went to graduate school to get a doctorate in clinical psychology, a woman from my Baptist church told me she thought it was a waste of time to study Freud instead of the Bible.

"Have you read many of his works?" I asked. She had not.

"Could you name even one thing he wrote?" She could not.

"Do you understand the difference between projection and reaction formation? Do you know the relationship between the conscience and the superego? Do you know his stages of psychosexual development?" She did not.

"Freud was a man who—regardless of whether anyone agrees with him—was one of the dominant shapers of twentieth-century thought. He was a writer and researcher and doctor; he won the Goethe Award for his literary influence on the German language; he read and wrote on biology and neurology and art and religion as well as psychology—and you feel competent to judge him when you can't even name a single monograph he penned?"

That was the last time my grandmother asked me about psychology.

I think of a bright young student who eventually found himself unable to believe in Christianity. Partly he was disillusioned by fellow Christians who "seemed happy to hide seri-

Many people, when they think of faith, think that it means choosing to believe when there is no good evidence. You cannot make yourself believe something through willpower.

146

ous problems in the Bible and in their arguments. They preferred comfort to intellectual honesty."

Many people, when they think of *faith*, think that it means choosing to believe when there is no good evidence. Mark Twain's definition of faith is "trying to believe what you know ain't so."

You cannot make yourself believe something through willpower. Oxford professor Richard Swinburne writes, "In general, a person cannot choose what to believe there and then. Belief is something that happens to a person, not something he or she does."

Sometimes people with "iffy" faith will think, *I have to try harder to believe that I'm going to get the answer that I want to my prayer.* It doesn't work. Trying hard to believe is toxic. It is a dangerous practice. I can say, "I'll try to learn. I'll try to study. I'll try to grow. I'll try to know God better. I'll try to pray." But I cannot directly generate belief through willpower.

Alice learned a lesson about the nature of beliefs on her trip to Wonderland. (Lewis Carroll was both an Oxford mathematician and an Anglican clergyman, so he was very interested in the nature of belief.) In the middle of a dizzying conversation, the Red Queen says to Alice, "Now I'll give you something to believe. I am 101 years, five months, and one day old."

This is too much for poor Alice. Although one would guess it is hard to gauge the age of an animated chess character, it is clear that the queen can't be beyond middle age.

"I can't believe that," said Alice.

"Can't you?" asked the queen, in a pitying tone. "Try again. Take a deep breath and shut your eyes."

Alice laughed. "There's no use trying," she said. "One can't believe impossible things."

"I daresay you haven't had much practice," said the queen. "When I was your age, I always did it for half an hour a day. Why, sometimes I believed as many as six impossible things before breakfast."

Philosopher Dallas Willard makes a provocative proposal: "Followers of Jesus are required to pursue truth wherever it leads them." This is perhaps a strange way to say it, but even more than we need to be committed to Jesus, we need to be committed to truth. For it is impossible to trust Jesus if way down deep inside, you don't think he was right. Sometimes believers are afraid that pursuing truth wherever it leads might make us uncomfortable. But as C. S. Lewis wrote, "Comfort is the one thing you cannot get by looking for it. If you look for truth, you may find comfort in the end: If you look for comfort, you will not get either comfort or truth—only soft soap and wishful thinking to begin with, and in the end, despair."

Jesus himself had quite a lot to say about truth. He said: "You will know the truth, and the truth will set you free" (John 8:32). "I am the way and the truth and the life" (14:6). "When he, the Spirit of truth, comes, he will guide you into all truth" (16:13).

Another way of saying this is, if you have to choose between Jesus and truth, choose truth. But according to Jesus, if you search for truth, you will find him. There is no other way to trust Jesus than to think and question and wrestle and struggle until you come to see that he really is true. One purpose of doubt is to motivate us to do that.

Uncertainty Produces Growth

As a parent, I have come to see the value of strategic uncertainty. My kids come to me and want the comfort of knowing. Will they get into that school or get that job, that prize? As a dad, what I want for them most is that they grow into really good people. And I recognize the "not knowing" eras are the biggest growth eras of all. If they can be poised and confident and care about other people even in the valley of uncertainty, they will grow more than they know. To be uncertain yet still care for others is maturity. To be uncertain and yet cheerful is to develop as a person.

148

Sometimes, as we saw earlier, we will have to make a 100 percent commitment to something even though we do not have 100 percent certainty in our beliefs about it. When we can live in the midst of uncertainty with joyful and courageous commitment, we will change. We will become, maybe not more certain, but more *faithful*. And faithfulness matters more than certainty. It just doesn't feel as good.

> There are times when a decision will require commitment when we don't have total certainty. For the most important decisions in life, this is almost always the case.

There are times when a decision will require commitment when we don't have total certainty. For the most important decisions in life, this is almost always the case. For example, let's say that before I get married, I think, *I'm human. I have no guarantees here, but I know that I want to marry this person. I'm 95 percent certain. I have a very low doubt level. But I'm finite, and that doubt is still there.*

Now imagine, when I was making my vows to Nancy — making my commitment — that I had said, "Nancy, I'm going to give you a good, solid 95 percent commitment in our marriage. I will be 95 percent faithful to you as we walk through life together." Do you think that would have flown with her? Not so much.

When you stand on that platform, when you make that vow, what you say is, "All that I am, all that I have, I thee endow. For better or worse, richer or poorer, in sickness and in health, I'll love and cherish — I'm all in."

What matters then is not certainty, but faithfulness. When certainty is not possible, faithfulness is still on the table.

This is true about the most important decision, the God decision. We don't have proof, but we have lots of good reasons. And one reason stands out over them all.

WHY I BELIEVE

My business is not to prove to any other man
that there is a God, but to find him for myself.
GEORGE MacDONALD

The majority of human beings who have ever lived would say that atheists Bertrand Russell, Christopher Hitchens, Richard Dawkins, Sam Harris, and Daniel Dennett are wrong. The best minds in the history of the human race — Plato, Augustine, Aquinas, Newton, Descartes, Leibniz, Pascal, Kierkegaard — thought that there were good reasons to believe there is a God. Since none of them are around to write out an explanation of why they believe, I will have to suffice.

And here is how I would like to lay it out. We will sift through a number of reasons to believe in God, looking for the one best reason.

G. K. Chesterton wrote:

If I am asked why I believe in Christianity, I can only answer, "for the same reason that an intelligent agnostic disbelieves in Christianity." I believe in it quite rationally upon the evidence.

But that evidence ... is not really in this or that alleged demonstration, it is in an enormous accumulation of small but unanimous facts. In fact, the secularist is not to be blamed because his objections to Christianity are miscellaneous and even scrappy; it is precisely such scrappy evidence that does convince the mind.

I believe there is a God for a pile of reasons: dreams, arguments, banana cream pie, umpires, *Hotel Rwanda*, complicated telephone mailbox systems, Little Nell, the happiness pill, and one other reason, one reason that trumps every other reason and leaves them all in the dust.

Scrappy enough for you?

These reasons for believing in God are not totally random. Some of them involve philosophical arguments that have technical names. All of them should be the object of careful reflection. But only one is the best.

Dreams

Last week I totaled my daughter's car. It split into two halves. I was trying to hold on to both halves, sliding down a hillside, when a large male deer approached me. He bit me gently on the hand. Then he went to get a small branch in his mouth. He was clearly going to whip me with it. An announcer was doing a kind of play-by-play of all this and said, "Well, it's all over now. When a deer comes after you with a switch, there is no hope...."

Then my alarm went off.

Dreams can be pretty weird. But I'm not sure they are any weirder than real life.

And to take an example from Philosophy 101, I cannot prove that my life is not a dream. Lao Tse asked the celebrated question, "If when I was asleep I was a man dreaming I was a butterfly, how

152

do I know when I am awake I am not a butterfly dreaming I am a man?" The writer of "Row, Row, Row Your Boat" was apparently in the Lao Tse camp. (Row gently, row merrily, life is but a dream.) I don't have *evidence* to disprove the butterfly theory, but I have a good *reason* not to believe it; and the reason is that if I don't believe I'm a real human being, I could miss out on my actual life. If I'm wrong, I haven't lost a lot, but if I'm right, I have a life. To demand doubt-free proof carries too high a price.

We all hold innumerable terribly important convictions that cannot be proven. For instance, you cannot prove that the past actually happened. You cannot prove that other people aren't really highly sophisticated robots. You cannot prove that it is wrong to torture innocent children. Alvin Plantinga, who is widely regarded as the premier philosopher of religion in our day, says that belief in God is something like this. It is what he calls a "basic conviction." We don't have ironclad *evidence* for these convictions, but we have good *reason* for believing them to be true. People may believe in God without being able to come up with syllogisms explaining why, but that doesn't mean their belief is irrational any more than to believe I'm awake is irrational. Belief in God is a properly basic conviction. But that is not the main reason I believe.

> *People may believe in God without being able to come up with syllogisms explaining why, but that doesn't mean their belief is irrational any more than to believe I'm awake is irrational.*

Arguments

I believe we have a moral code in our hearts and that Somebody put it there. This idea comes by way of C. S. Lewis.

Pay attention the next time you hear an argument. Maybe you can go start one just to check this out. Nancy and I had a good argument recently about which one of us was supposed to buy a clock radio for me. Surprisingly, I lost.

When people argue, here are the kinds of things they say:

"I do way more than my fair share of work around this house, and you do way too little!" We call those people husbands and wives.

"He got a bigger piece of dessert. He got a bigger allowance! He did fewer chores. He got a later curfew time than I did, and it's not fair!" We call those people brothers and sisters.

"You're a miserable boss, and this is a dysfunctional sweat shop, and I am grossly overworked and criminally underpaid." We call those people unemployed.

When we argue, we don't just say, "Do what I want because I'm stronger and I can make you do it." We say things like, "That's not right! That's not good! You're not being fair!" In other words, we appeal to a standard that is independent and objective and higher than you and I. We appeal to the idea that there is such a thing as right and wrong.

In theory, many people in our day hold the belief that right and wrong are subjective — just preference, just vanilla and chocolate. You have yours, and I have mine. Everybody is different. Author Dinesh D'Souza points out that in our society we will often hear someone say, "Don't impose your beliefs on me."

D'Souza says he finds it interesting that we don't say, "Don't impose your geometry on me. Don't impose your chemistry on me." Why don't we hear such things? Because we assume that science and mathematics are about objective reality. We don't think they can be "imposed" on us. But we often believe that morals and values are simply subjective preferences. You have yours. I have mine. Everything is arbitrary. Whenever you hear two people argue about whether something is right or wrong, it shows we know that right or wrong isn't subjective. Deep down we all live on the assumption that moral reality is built into the way life is.

This is exactly what Paul was writing about when he said that "the requirements of the law [what's right and what's wrong] are written on [people's] hearts." We can't get away from this. When we argue, we show that we know this. Paul continues, "their consciences also bearing witness, and their thoughts now accusing, now even defending them" (Romans 2:15).

Every human being knows two things: *There is a way we ought to behave.* We do not invent this code; we only discover it. We might be fuzzy on the details of it sometimes, but we have a general idea of what it is. We also know that *we don't live up to this standard.* We all fall short. We need forgiveness. We need grace. We need to get fixed.

Every time people argue, they are implying that the universe is not an accident, that there is a moral order built into the way things are, because it was put there by Somebody, and that Somebody is God. The good news is that he is a gracious God. That's part of why I believe in God. But it's not the main reason.

Banana Cream Pie

I had a philosophy professor in college named Steve Evans, and although I often couldn't keep up with him, he made one statement I have never forgotten: one of the greatest proofs of the existence of God is banana cream pie. It's kind of a shorthand version of the claim that we can reason from the existence of creation to the existence of a Creator.

What is convincing to me about that is not simply the complexity of creation. I know some people argue that the complexity of, for example, the human eye can only be explained by a creator. For me, complexity does not get to the root of the matter. And I get a little concerned about a "God of the gaps" approach that

> What is convincing to me is not so much the complexity of creation as the goodness of creation. Even the ugliness we see — cancer and pollution and slums — are painful precisely because creation is so good when it is right.

requires science or natural selection to be unable to account for something in order to prove God. What if down the road science figures it out?

No, what is convincing to me is not so much the *complexity* of creation as the *goodness* of creation. If there is no God, then it really doesn't matter if anything exists or not. But there is another way of viewing things: "God spoke, and it was so, and God saw that it was good." Even the ugliness we see — cancer and pollution and slums — are painful precisely because creation is so good when it is right. The goodness of creation is a reason to believe. But it is not the greatest reason.

Umpires

One time during the off season, an umpire in a softball league in Colorado got stopped by a cop for speeding. He pleaded for mercy, explained that he was a very good driver, and told why he had to be in a hurry. The officer wasn't buying the umpire's argument. "Tell it to the judge," he said.

When softball season rolled around, the umpire was umpiring his first game. The first batter to come up happened to be the cop who ticketed him for speeding. They recognized each other. It was awkward for the officer.

"So, how did the thing with the ticket go?" the officer asked.

"Better swing at everything," the umpire replied.

We have a desire for justice, not just for things to work out the way we want them. We all are umpires. We can't help it. Aristotle called this ability *phronesis*, the capacity to see moral, relevant features of a particular case and make good judgments. And this capacity is tied to the way things ought to be. We have a conviction that for life to make sense, for existence to be rational, justice must prevail. Therefore, people who fight for justice are not being arbitrary; they are working for the way things are supposed to be.

Our demand for justice tells us that there must be a Judge, that justice must one day prevail. And the greatest voices of justice who ever lived, the Hebrew prophets who called their nation to justice as no nation had ever been called before, insisted that one day justice will prevail. It will roll on like a river (Amos 5:24). Our thirst for justice tells us there is a God. But it is not the most convincing voice I hear about God.

Hotel Rwanda

I first saw the movie *Hotel Rwanda* with my daughter and a group of her friends. In Rwanda, in the space of less than a year, a million people were destroyed, many of them butchered with machetes, for belonging to the wrong tribe. After the movie we went out and talked for a long time, trying to absorb what we had seen. A year or so later I got to meet in real life the central man the film was about, and his dignity and courage are convicting.

Of course, in one sense the problem of evil poses one of the greatest difficulties—for me the greatest—to believing in God. Why he does not stop it is something I don't fully understand.

However, this is another angle. Of all forms of suffering, the worst is that which involves human wickedness. Nazi Germany, Cambodia, and Rwanda are some of our deepest horror stories. But it's hard to see how there could be such a thing as *wickedness* if naturalism is true. The category of wickedness makes sense only if people were created and intended to behave a certain way. An accidental universe may have pleasure and pain, but there would be no *moral* distinction between them, since wickedness can exist only in a moral universe. The reality of evil—not just pain, but evil—is a reason to believe. But it's not the greatest reason.

Telephone Mailbox Systems

We are creatures who blame each other. Nancy and I have a magnet on our refrigerator that reads, "I didn't say it was your fault. I said I was going to *blame* you." But blame has something to tell us about our nature.

Quite a few years ago I was in my office talking with someone. I paused a moment to leave a message on someone's voicemail. (I was using the speaker phone to leave the message rather than picking up the receiver.) And the person whose voicemail I was calling was one of the nicest people I knew.

I don't know why, but after I hung up the phone, I started to speak to the person who was in my office about the person for whom I had left the voice message, using a mocking tone of voice—"what a *nice* person X is ... always being *so sweet....*" I wasn't making bad things up. But instead of speaking about the person in an admiring way, I made it sound as if the person's niceness was naive or innocent or artificial. Just to get a laugh. Or maybe just to make me feel better about not having that level of kindness in my life.

All of a sudden I heard a dial tone coming over the loudspeaker. I realized that all I had said had been recorded on that person's answering machine. The person would hear every ugly word.

I got ill. Physically sick to my stomach. I had to go to the office of the person I had spoken about and try to explain why I had done something so cutting that I could not even understand it myself.

To this day I can't think of that moment without feeling it in my stomach a little. Paul said our consciences "bear witness" (Romans 2:15) that we are moral beings in a spiritually meaningful universe. I had no one else to blame.

Accountability for actions makes sense only in a universe of persons. Naturalism says that human beings are just a collection of atoms. Some people believe that Darwin showed that human beings may be different in degree but not in kind from any other creatures. The Bible, however, says that humans are a different *kind* of being, and that we are made in the image of God—possessors of souls. In our hearts, we know this to be true about ourselves.

The following illustration, though a bit odd, tells one of the ways we know we are unique creatures: we never put an animal on trial. When someone is bitten by a lion, when somebody gets mauled by a bear, when someone lives in a sick codependent relationship with a cat (and my own conviction as a dog guy is that all cat owners live in sick codependent relationships with their cats), we don't put that animal on trial. We don't sue it. We don't take it to court. We just say, "That's its nature. That's the nature of a bear. That's the nature of a lion. That's simply the product of its nature and its training. That's all it is." (Actually, a group of fishermen in Hartlepool, England, who feared a French invasion during the Napoleonic wars apparently tried and hanged a monkey on the charge of being a French spy, but the British have been embarrassed about it ever since, which only confirms the larger point.)

We put human beings on trial because human beings are not just products of instinct and training; we are moral agents. We are "blameworthy." And our transgressions require something more costly than just education, therapy, or closure. (A friend of mine says one difference between a therapist and an AA sponsor is that the only time a sponsor says, "Closure," is before the word *mouth*.)

Thoroughgoing naturalism says that people do not have a moral nature. They

> We put human beings on trial because we are not just products of instinct and training; we are moral agents. Our transgressions require something more costly than education, therapy, or closure.

are not free. They are just products of causes and forces. It's just that we don't know all the details yet. But nobody raises a child believing that. Nobody makes a friend believing that. We know better. The practice of blaming tells us there is a God. But this is not the greatest reason to believe.

Little Nell

Charles Dickens was a rock star in his day. He wrote serialized novels that would be published one chapter at a time, and whole countries would come to a standstill when a new chapter emerged. One of his most famous (and infamous) heart-wrenching scenes was the death of Little Nell in *The Old Curiosity Shop*. His critics charged him with hypersentimentalism. (Oscar Wilde, in a typically cynical moment, said that you'd have to have a heart of stone to read the death scene of Little Nell without laughing.) But most of Dickens's readers were brokenhearted. Thousands sobbed when they read it.

There is no more amazing *fact* in the universe than the existence of human persons. Why do firefighters risk their lives to save a single little girl in a burning building? Because individual persons matter. The shortfall of evolution — in its atheist form — is its failure to attach importance to a single individual. In the Christian story, each part of creation matters because it is prized by God. A hen is more than just the vehicle through which one egg gets another egg. And human beings matter most of all.

Human nature is such an extraordinary thing, unprecedented in the universe. G. K. Chesterton said that one of the reasons he became convinced about Christianity is because it captures the fullness and the mystery and the contradiction and the paradox of life — especially of persons. He said that there are some approaches, such as stoicism, that are pessimistic about human nature, but that certain forms of humanism teach that "man is the measure of all things" and have an exalted, optimistic view of human nature.

When it comes to human nature, Christianity is not just pessimistic or optimistic or blandly "middle of the road." It is wildly pessimistic: "The heart is deceitful above all things and beyond cure" (Jeremiah 17:9). And it is wildly optimistic and hopeful: "Dear friends, now we are children of God, and what we will be has not yet been made known" (1 John 3:2).

Christianity grasps all this truth and wonder and mystery and darkness and potential for goodness in the human condition. No one put it better than Pascal: "What kind of freak then is man? How novel, how monstrous, how chaotic, how paradoxical, how prodigious! Judge of all things, feeble earthworm, repository of truth, sink of doubt and error, glory and refuse of the universe."

One of the problems with doubt is that once you deny the existence of God and the existence of spiritual truth, once reality is reduced to atoms and quarks, it's not just God who disappears; the whole idea of *persons* begins to fade.

Steven Pinker, a philosopher of science at Yale, writes that we are only our brain functions. The classic concept of what it means to be a person is illusion. There is no such thing as the mind. The human brain is only an ingeniously assembled computer. There is no such thing as the self. The self is just another network of brain systems. There is no *soul*. There is no centered moral agent responsible for actions. There are only synapses firing. There is no *you*. There is no me. There is no Steve Pinker.

And maybe he's right. But somebody keeps cashing Steve Pinker's royalty checks.

One of the great tests of any worldview is, what does it have to say to a dying person? And I do not know what naturalism has to say to a dying nine-year-old girl other than, "Sorry. Tough luck." The survival of the species cannot mean much if the survival of individuals is meaningless.

I believe there is a God partly because I believe there is a you. You are an individual who matters. *You* are a reason to believe in God. But you are not the best reason.

The Happiness Pill

I believe the existence of joy points toward God.

Sometimes people think that what we really want more than anything else is to be happy. If you ask people, "What is the number one desire of the human race?" the answer would probably be "Happiness." We say we want to be happy above everything else.

I do not think that is true, and I'll tell you why. Let's say that there is a pill, which, if you swallowed it, would put you into a permanent coma. In this coma you would have thrilling dreams. You would have uninterrupted happiness surges. You would have pleasure, delight, and joy forever. You would be asleep and never in touch with anybody, but you would have never-ending happiness. Would you take that pill? *No!*

Imagine that you could plug your brain into an outlet, and it would stimulate your pleasure center forever so that you would feel great pleasure throughout all eternity, but you would never *do* anything. You would never go anywhere. You would never know anyone. Would you do it? *No!* You wouldn't do it, and it would be a nightmare if someone did it to you, because what you want is something deeper than joy. Joy, although we love it, always points us beyond ourselves.

> *We want something deeper than joy. Joy, although we love it, always points us beyond ourselves.*

We want joy in beauty. That is why a scene, a mountaintop, or music sometimes pierces our hearts. We want joy in noble thoughts. We want joy in getting lost in a great cause that sets things right and brings happiness to others. We want joy in a person.

All will be well,
And all will be well,
And all manner of things will be well.
JULIAN OF NORWICH

We read, C. S. Lewis says in *Shadowlands*, to know that we are not alone. We read because we want to know if there is a reason to believe. And sometimes when we read, someone names a truth that resonates so deeply inside us that we find ourselves laughing or crying because we never knew there was a name for what we hoped.

One of those passages, for me, comes at the end of G. K. Chesterton's book *Orthodoxy*. It is a picture of God and the destiny of his creation so good that we can hardly hope it will be true. It produces maybe a sliver of what happened to the disciples after the resurrection, when we are told, "They still did not believe it because of joy and amazement" (Luke 24:41).

If what Jesus taught is true, then joy is at the core of the universe. If Jesus was wrong, if unbelief is right, then joy and the hunger for it is an accident. Then the earth is a ball of dirt and water floating for a few seconds in a cosmic chamber destined to perish when the Big Bang collapses in on itself. "What is it all but a trouble of ants in the gleam of a million million suns?" asked Tennyson.

If Jesus is right, joy was at the beginning, was challenged in the middle, and will be restored at the end. If he was wrong, joy is a momentary illusion that was absent in the beginning and will soon be forever stilled.

I believe Jesus was right. I believe joy is as real as Cleveland.

Orthodoxy closes with a picture of Jesus and the hope of joy that still slays me when I read it. Especially the last line. Especially the last word. But it requires a little context, and since I don't have space enough here to print the whole book, I'll try to set it up.

Imagine you have a five-year-old child whom you love very much. Let us say this child has been sick, and you are afraid you might lose her. Then the doctors tell you that she can have an operation. It is in fact a very simple one—like having her tonsils out. It will be without risk. She will live, they say. She'll be fine. Your joy knows no limits.

But your five-year-old child is scared to death. She is dreading the operation. She is frightened by the surgeon. She does not yet know that all will be well. You try to reassure her, but she doesn't yet understand. So you cannot let her see the lightness of your heart. You can't joke around. You can't laugh. She would think you didn't care. You must take her fear seriously. You must let her know you empathize. But every once in a while, you have to leave her sickroom. You have to be able to laugh because you know all will be well.

> The joy of the Lord is not that you are happy when you go to church. It is the joy that will come one day when you finally see face-to-face, clear as crystal, that for which you were made.

What if the human condition is something like this? What if Julian of Norwich is right? The apostle John says that one day "God himself will be with them and be their God. He will wipe every tear from their eyes. There will be no more death or mourning or crying or pain, for the old order of things has passed away" (Revelation 21:3–4). What if that is actually the way things are going to be? What if all things are going to be well? What if Jesus knew this? Really knew?

Then everything would have looked different to him. God would be the parent, and we would be the five-year-old in the sickroom. And God would have to accommodate himself to us; he would have to knit his brow and nod his head and take our fear seriously. But every once in a while God would have to excuse himself just to go outside and laugh.

Now, with that picture in mind, here are the final words of Chesterton's book:

Joy, which was the small publicity of the pagan, is the gigantic secret of the Christian. And as I close this chaotic volume, I open again the strange small book from which all Christianity came; and I am again haunted by a kind of confirmation. The tremendous figure which fills the Gospels towers in this respect, as in every other, above all the thinkers who ever thought themselves tall. His pathos was natural, almost casual. The Stoics, ancient and modern, were proud of concealing their tears. He never concealed his tears; he showed them plainly on his open face at any daily sight, such as the far sight of his native city. Yet he concealed something. Solemn supermen and imperial diplomatists are proud of restraining their anger. He never restrained his anger. He flung furniture down the front steps of the temple and asked men how they expected to escape the damnation of hell. Yet he restrained something. I say it with reverence; there was in that shattering personality a thread that must be called shyness. There was something that he hid from all men when he went up a mountain to pray. There was something that he covered constantly by abrupt silence or impetuous isolation. There was some one thing that was too great for God to show us when he walked upon our earth; and I have sometimes fancied that it was his mirth.

The joy of the Lord is not that you are happy when you go to church or when you're singing hymns or when you're quoting Bible verses. It is the joy that will come one day when you finally see face-to-face, clear as crystal, that for which you were made. That secret longing that you have carried with you like a wound your whole life long will be met. That is not the best reason for believing. But it's getting us close.

Once there was a Man who had that joy. People saw him.

People knew him. One time he said to his friends, "I have told you [how to remain in my love] so that my joy may be in you and that your joy may be complete" (John 15:11). Our quest for joy, our broken, messed-up, obsessive, endless pursuit of joy tells us we were made for the Joy-Bringer.

Now I will say what I think is the best reason for believing.

Jesus Believed

There is simply no one more worth trusting that Jesus. There is no one whose understanding of life has come close to his. There is no one who affected history like him. There is simply no other source — no book, no guru, no hunch, no personal experience — worth betting the farm on. As Elton Trueblood so well said, "A Christian is a person who, with all the honesty of which he is capable, becomes convinced that the fact of Jesus Christ is the most trustworthy that he knows in his entire universe of discourse."

And Jesus said there is a God. George MacDonald wrote, "I can only say with my whole heart that I hope we have indeed a Father in heaven; but this man says *he knows*."

Jesus is in the life-changing business. From the very beginning all kinds of people were drawn to him and would come to him — satisfied people, messed-up people, lepers and injured people, forgotten people, despised people, prostitutes, tax collectors, admired people, wealthy people, religious leaders. There was something about this man Jesus that made their hearts cave in and then be born again.

A proud, vindictive, violent, arrogant, self-occupied religious leader named Saul of Tarsus was traveling down the road when suddenly he had a vision of Jesus. As a matter of historical record, he became Paul — a different man with a different name, whose mind, writings, love for people, and self-sacrificial gift of his life to the world were so compelling that human minds are still fascinated by him two thousand years later. People devote their lives to studying what he wrote. How did that life get changed? The evidence of lives changed by Jesus is so abundant that the full story can never be told. It can never be matched. Not by any culture, by any book, by any program, by any hero.

I have never heard anybody say, "One day I realized there was no God, no one behind reality, no life after death. I realized existence is a meaningless accident, begun by chance and destined for oblivion, and it changed my life. I used to be addicted to alcohol, but now the 'law of natural selection' has set me free. I used to be greedy, but now the story of the Big Bang has made me generous. I used to be afraid, but now random chance has made me brave."

I have never heard the story of an accidental, meaningless universe changing a life like that. Now, I have heard people say they were oppressed by the form of faith they followed and felt a sense of liberation when they didn't believe it was true anymore. But I have never seen anyone receive the power to live the kind of life and become the kind of person he or she wants to be by hearing that there is no story behind the universe. I have never heard anyone say, "Now I have found a meaningful existence from a meaningless reality."

> *I have never heard anybody say, "I used to be greedy, but now the story of the Big Bang has made me generous. I used to be afraid, but now random chance has made me brave."*

But Jesus has been doing that for two thousand years.

A guy by the name of Bill Moore, who grew up in poverty, got drunk one time and shot a man for five thousand dollars. He ended up on death row. Lee Strobel met Bill and writes about him in his book *The Case for Faith*.

A couple of guys went into prison (because God prompts people to go into prisons) and told him, "Bill, there is a man, Jesus, who loves you, and he gave his life on a cross. He died for you. He went to death row for you." Nobody had ever told Bill about Jesus before. He'd been sitting on death row for years. He turned his life over to Jesus, and it changed him so much—changed the darkness and bitterness and hatred inside him so much—that other people began to be drawn to him. People started meeting Jesus through this guy on death row. He became known as "The Peacemaker." His cell block was the safest place in the penitentiary because so many people were coming to Christ through Bill Moore.

Churches found out about this, and when people needed counseling, no kidding, churches started sending people to the penitentiary to get counseling from Bill Moore. Can you imagine calling a church to ask for a referral and hearing, "I want you to go over to death row. There's an inmate there...." What does that? Jesus does that.

Bill Moore was changed so much that he won the love of the family of the man he killed. It changed him so much over the sixteen-year period that all kinds of people wrote letters for him. Eventually, the authorities not only canceled his death sentence; they not only commuted his sentence, which was unprecedented; but they paroled him. Bill Moore now serves as head of congregation in a couple of housing projects in a desperately poor area. When Strobel met with him, he asked, "Bill, what in the world turned your life around? Was it a new medication? Was it some kind of rehab program? Was it a new approach to counseling?"

Bill said, "No, Lee, it wasn't any of that stuff. It was Jesus Christ."

Atheism really has nothing to say to a guy on death row. Because when you're living on death row (and we're all living on death row), there's really only one thing you want to know.

THE CATCHER

I just cannot read the Gospel story without knowing
that I am being sought out in love, being called
to life's most sacred task, being offered life's highest prize....
But I am not now arguing. I am only confessing.

JOHN BAILLIE

There are three moves in the "leap of faith": letting go of the trapeze — whatever your trapeze is, waiting, and then being caught. Letting go, waiting, being caught.

The Daring Young Man

Jesus comes to this earth and actually lives this way. He lets go of life in heaven. He lets go of the glory. He lets go of the power. He lets go of the riches. And he is born in a little stable to obscure, impoverished parents. He grows up in a blue-collar family, working as a carpenter. He has an itinerant ministry as a homeless rabbi. Then, finally, he lets go of his ministry and lets go of his disciples.

The word *trapeze* — the little bar between the ropes that a trapeze artist has to let go of—comes from the ancient Greek *trapeza*, meaning table. About the only time it is used in the New Testament is when the writer claims that Jesus gathers his friends around the table, the *trapeza*, what we now call the Communion table, and teaches them that he will have to let go of his life for them and that the only way to hang on to one's life is to let it go. Then he climbs the cross and lets go. He hangs above the earth for three hours with his hands stretched out, not moving a muscle.

"Father, into your hands I commend my spirit," he breathed.

When he did that, he was saving us, and he was teaching us about trust.

Here's the leap: God comes to you and says, "Let go. Will you let go?"

God came to Abraham and said, "Let go of everything familiar. Let go of your family, your home, and your culture, and go where I tell you to go. Will you do that? Will you let go?"

Jesus came to a rich young ruler one day. He loved him, and he said, "Will you let go of your trapeze?" The rich ruler's trapeze was called "money." "Will you give away all your possessions or sell them and give the money to the poor and come follow me?"

Jesus spoke to a woman caught in an adulterous affair. He said, "Go and sin no more." Will you let go of that relationship that you know dishonors God?

What are you to let go of? Anything that will keep you from God.

Let go of that relationship if it dishonors God.

Let go of your attachment to money.

Let go of your power; be a servant.

Let go of your addiction. Admit it. Get help.

Let go of that habit.

Let go of that grudge.

Let go of your ego, your pride, your money, your reputation, your disobedience.

God will come and say, "Let go."
Then he says, "Wait."

Nail Picking

Nobody likes to wait.

Waiting is the in-between time when I have responded to God but things are not yet the way I want them to be. And I keep obeying. And I keep on trusting. And I keep saying yes and hold out my hands. "God, I can't make things turn out the way I want them to be. I don't have control."

The flyer can do nothing.

What do you do while you wait? Personally, I pick at my nails. It's a bad habit, I know. But I have so many worse ones that on the scale of my habits it comes close to being a charming eccentricity. I have raised it to nearly an art form. Thumb hangnails work best, then the index and middle finger. I pretty much never go after the last two fingers unless the first three are all under repair.

Nail picking is an example of what used to be called a nervous habit or self-soothing behavior. I tell myself I could stop anytime. I tell myself it's just something I do to help myself think. But the more stressed out I am, the more thinking my fingers seem to need to do. If I'm worried about one of my kids, my nails become a kind of agnostic rosary of anxiety. When something is not going well, the nail picking accelerates. I'm doing it right now.

> Waiting is the in-between time when I have responded to God but things are not yet the way I want them to be. I keep obeying. I keep on trusting. And I keep holding out my hands.

Nail picking is what the Israelites did as they whined their way across the desert waiting forty years for the Promised Land. It is what Gideon did early in the morning when he went out to check the fleece to see if God meant business or was just another smooth talker. It is what occupied the disciples Good Friday afternoon to Easter Sunday morning.

I worry while I wait, and my fingers torture each other to keep my mind distracted. They are tiny, mute little disfigured sentinels crying out my lack of faith. *I believe, help my doubting fingers.* So I sometimes take comfort in a nail picker named Abraham. Abraham stands as the great example of faith in the New Testament. He is talked about in the books of Romans, Galatians, and Hebrews.

God makes a promise, then tells Abraham to leave home and go where God will guide him.

Ben Patterson tells of a common experience of westerners, particularly missionaries, traveling through jungle sections of the Amazon. They will ask members of a village to give them directions to where they want to go. "I have a compass, a map, and some coordinates."

The villager knows precisely the directions to get them there, but he offers to take them himself.

"No, that's okay. I don't want a guide. I just want directions."

"That's no good. I must take you there."

"But I have a map right here. And I have a compass. And the coordinates."

"It does not work that way. I can get you there, but I must take you myself. You must follow me."

We prefer directions, principles, steps, keys. We prefer these things because they leave us in control. If I'm holding the map, I'm still in charge of the trip. I can go where I want to go. If I have a guide, I must trust. I must follow. I must relinquish control.

God is not much on maps and compasses and coordinates. Life just doesn't work that way. We don't need directions. We need a Guide.

God tells Abraham that he is going to be a father and eventually a great nation, that he is going to have a son by Sarah. Then

Abraham has to wait. Know how long Abraham waits? Twenty-four years. How well does he do at waiting, trusting, and obeying? Not so well.

Abraham takes his wife, Sarah, to Egypt, and says to his wife, "Sarah, you're a beautiful woman. When Pharaoh sees you, he's going to want you for his harem. He might kill me to get to you, so let's just pretend that you're my sister. That way, if he takes you into his harem, I'll still be okay."

This is not "Husband of the Year" material. But it works, so years later Abraham actually does it again. Years later he still has no son, and he is upset about it. So Sarah says to him, "Here's my maid. Why don't you just sleep with her and have a son that way?" Abraham says, "Okay, honey. If you think that's a good idea, I'll do that." Just a little passive at that point, isn't he?

Abraham's actions lead to a big mess. Years later God comes to Abraham again and says, "You will have a son." Does Abraham receive these words with faith? Genesis 17:17 says, "Abraham fell facedown; he laughed and said to himself, 'Will a son be born to a man a hundred years old?'"

God says to Abraham, "I'm going to give you a son," and Abraham laughs at him. He falls down laughing.

Just a note here: we are often tempted to think, "If I could have one miracle—one supernatural event in my life the way they had them in biblical times—then I would know for sure. Then I would never doubt."

I don't know how it is that God came to Abraham, but regardless of how it happened, God came to Abraham in such a way that there was still room for doubt. That happened often—with Moses, with Gideon, and with many others.

God comes again to Abraham (Genesis 18). This time he is outside of his tent, and Sarah is inside. God says, "I will surely return to you about this time next year, and Sarah your wife will have a son." Abraham, at this point, is very old. Look at what the text says: "Sarah laughed to herself as she thought, 'After I am worn out and my master is old, will I now have this pleasure?'"

"Then the Lord said to Abraham, 'Why did Sarah laugh and say, "Will I really have a child, now that I am old?" Is anything too hard for the Lord?'"

I love this little conversation. "Sarah was afraid, so she lied and said, 'I did not laugh.'"

But the Lord said, "Yes, you did laugh."

They sound like two little kids going at it:

"Did not!"

"Did so!"

God and Sarah bickering like two seven-year-olds.

That's waiting. Abraham doesn't wait very well. Doubts. Impregnates Hagar and then kicks her and his son out. *Let's go.* Waits, but not well. Then, after years and years and years and years, he's caught. Big hands. God comes. God answers his prayer.

Sarah finds out one day, after years and years, that she is pregnant. Can you imagine that day? Imagine how she tells Abraham.

Regardless of how it happened, God came to Abraham in such a way that there was still room for doubt. That happened often — with Moses, with Gideon, and with many others.

Can you imagine how they laugh? A woman that age getting pregnant? She gave birth to a son, and they named him Isaac. Do you know what Isaac means? "He laughs." They named the boy "He laughs."

Sarah said, "God has brought me laughter, and everyone who hears about this will laugh with me" (Genesis 21:6).

They will laugh at a baby being born in a neonatal unit and Medicare picking up the tab. They will laugh because Sarah will be the only one in the grocery store buying Pampers and Depends for the same family; because they are all eating Gerber baby food since there is not a single tooth in the family; because when they go out for a walk, everybody uses a walker.

They will laugh because they waited so badly, because they misbehaved, because they deceived and doubted the whole time and God showed up anyway.

This is the laughter of faith in God.

It is worth asking—if there is no God—what is there to laugh about? Jean-Paul Sartre has a story about this, about the kind of laughter he finds in a world where God and meaning are dead. It is a kind of parable meant to explain that a human being's best efforts are doomed to failure in the end, that death and nothingness will win out. A man is threatened with death if he does not betray his friend by telling his captors his friend's location. He refuses. They beat him. He sends them on a wild goose chase by telling them his friend is someplace where he knows his friend is not. By a wild chance, when his captors go to the place, his friend happens to be there, and they find him and capture him and kill him.

The man is given his freedom. Sartre ends the story by saying that the man laughed until he cried. In spite of our best intentions, life is a cruel joke, and the joke is on us. Sartre said of himself toward the end of his life, "Atheism is a cruel and long-range affair. I think I've carried it through."

But in the Abraham story, the laughter and the tears are finally all joy.

You let go, and you wait, and you get caught. The flyer can do nothing. The Catcher does everything. God is calling, "Trust me. All will be well. Let go. Let go. Let go."

The Only Way

There is no way to God that bypasses the call to let go. You may have many intellectual doubts, and it is really important to be honest about those, to talk about them and study. However, thinking and studying alone never remove the need to choose. The question of faith is never just an intellectual decision. This comes only when you say, "I'll start with something that Jesus said that I think is true, and I'll actually do what he says. I'll actually let go." And then you wait.

I marvel at the last words used to describe the disciples in the gospel of Matthew—our last glimpse of men who followed Jesus for three years, learned from him, and saw him crucified and resurrected: "Then the eleven disciples went to ... the mountain where Jesus had told them to go. When they saw him, they worshiped him; but some doubted" (Matthew 28:16–17).

This is an amazing picture. They have seen him, listened to him, followed him, studied him, and seen him crucified and resurrected—and the last thing we read about them is *"and some doubted."* Matthew doesn't cover this up. He points it out.

Biblical scholar Frederick Dale Bruner says, "The Christian faith is bi-polar. Disciples live their life between worship and doubt, trusting and questioning, hoping and worrying."

Then Jesus gives the disciples what is called the Great Commission, sends them out to be his agents in the world. Jesus looks at these worshiping doubters and says: "You go! You doubters, go. You risk your lives for me. You change your world for me. And you will find as you go that it is your own doubts that are healed. You doubters are included too."

Disciples are not people who never doubt. They doubt and worship. They doubt and serve. They doubt and help each other with their doubts. They doubt and practice faithfulness. They doubt and wait for their doubt one day to be turned to knowing.

Waiting is really hard. Maybe you're not sure if you can wait for God anymore. But if you do not believe Jesus, if you do not wait for the Father whom Jesus himself believed in, then the question becomes, what will you wait for? We're all waiting for something, whether we want to or not. We're all waiting—in our own lives, in our sorry world. If it's not for God — for the Catcher — then what is it for?

It seems ironic that nearly every kid, at some point in his or her life, wants to run away and join the circus. The truth is that we are all born holding on to a trapeze — a little trapeze we call our "life." We hold on to it tightly: our security, our "okay-ness," our success, our importance, our worth, our stuff, our bodies, our health, our influence.

Then Jesus comes along and says: "You can let go of all that. You can let go of your life, because Someone is holding it. You can die to all the things that would keep you from living in my kingdom, and you'll find out that you haven't died to anything at all that matters. Let go.

"Let go of all the darkness.

"Let go of all the selfishness.

"Let go of all the fear.

"Just let go."

Believe him or not. One day — maybe tomorrow, maybe next year, maybe fifty years from now — you will let go of this little trapeze called your "life," and so will I. One day you will take your last breath, and your hands will go slack, and the trapeze will fall from your hands. The real question is what happens then?

> *Disciples are not people who never doubt. They doubt and worship, doubt and serve, doubt and help each other with their doubts. They wait for their doubt one day to be turned to knowing.*

Some believe that is the end. No safety net. Some believe that the neurons that you mistakenly believe add up to a soul will just stop firing on that day. The six trillion atoms that were employed by your body will find positions somewhere else, and the universe will neither know nor care.

But Jesus believed there is a Catcher, and he does not have sweaty hands.

SOURCES

Chapter 1. Faith, Doubt, and Being Born

15: Wolfgang von Goethe, quoted in James Crenshaw, *Old Testament Wisdom* (Louisville: Westminster John Kfnox Press, 1998), 184.

19: *The Brothers Karamazov*, in The Great Books, vol. 52 (New York: Encyclopedia Britannica), 1952.

20: Elie Wiesel, *Night* (New York: Hill and Wang, 1987), 43.

21: André Comte-Sponville, *A Short Treatise on the Great Virtues* (New York: Vintage, 2001), 148.

21: Daniel C. Dennett, *Breaking the Spell: Religion as a Natural Phenomenon* (New York: Viking, 2006), 7.

22: Sam Harris, *Letter to a Christian Nation* (New York: Knopf, 2006), 88.

22: Christopher Hitchens, *God Is Not Great: How Religion Poisons Everything* (New York: Twelve, 2007).

22: Richard Dawkins, *The God Delusion* (New York: Houghton Mifflin, 2006), 31.

23: Michael Novak, *Belief and Unbelief* (New Brunswick, N.J.: Transaction, 2006), 7.

23: Jennifer Hecht, *Doubt: A History: The Great Doubters and Their Legacy of Innovation from Socrates and Jesus to Thomas Jefferson and Emily Dickinson* (New York: HarperCollins, 2003), xi.

23: Gary Wolf, "The Church of the Non-believers," *Wired* (February 20, 2007).

24: Martin Seligman, *Authentic Happiness* (New York: Free Press, 2002), 287.

24: Billy Graham, TV interview, *Prime Time Live*, ABC network, aired May 22, 2000.

24: Martin Luther, *Luther's Works*, vol. 54 (Philadelphia: Fortress, 1957), 453.

24: Elie Wiesel, quoted in Antonio Monda, *Do You Believe?* (New York: Vintage, 2007), 71.

25: Nicholas Wolterstorff, *Lament for a Son* (Grand Rapids: Eerdmans, 1987), 66.

26: Ibid., 68.

Chapter 2. Why Bother?

27: Martin Luther, quoted in Alister McGrath, *Doubting* (Downers Grove, Ill.: InterVarsity Press, 2006), 26.

28: William Clifford, "The Ethics of Belief," in Gerald D. McCarthy, *The Ethics of Belief Debate*, 9th ed. (Atlanta: Scholars, 1986), 14.

29: Thomas Huxley, cited in Jennifer Hecht, *Doubt: A History: The Great Doubters and Their Legacy of Innovation from Socrates and Jesus to Thomas Jefferson and Emily Dickinson* (New York: HarperCollins, 2003), 407.

29: William James, *The Will to Believe* (New York: Longmans, Green, 1987), 10ff.

31: Lesslie Newbigin, *Proper Confidence* (Grand Rapids: Eerdmans, 1995), 23–24.

31: Woody Allen, quoted in www.great-quotes.com/cgi-bin/author.cgi?letter=A.

33: Yann Martel, *Life of Pi* (New York: Harcourt, 2001), 28.

34: James Conner, *Pascal's Wager* (New York: HarperCollins, 2006), 2.

35: Ibid., 38.

35: Vladimir Nabakov, quoted in Jim Holt, "Eternity for Atheists," *New York Times* (July 29, 2007), 11.

36: Hecht, *Doubt*, x–xi.

36: Michael Novak, *Belief and Unbelief* (New Brunswick, N.J.: Transaction, 2006), xxi.

36: Henri Nouwen, *Sabbatical Journey* (New York: Crossroad, 1998), 40, 74–75.

Chapter 3. What Kind of Belief Really Matters?

39: Madeleine L'Engle, quoted in Lynn Anderson, *If I Really Believe, Why Do I Have All These Doubts?* (Minneapolis: Bethany House, 1992), 61.

40: Daniel Dennett, cited in Wikipedia, s.v. "belief," http://en.wikipedia.org/wiki/Belief.

40: *The Lord of the Rings: Fellowship of the Ring*, motion picture, Universal Studios, directed by Peter Jackson, 2001.

41: Robert Fulghum, *Everything I Need to Know I Learned in Kindergarten* (New York: Villiard, 1987).

41: *Bull Durham*, motion picture, produced by Thom Mount, written and directed by Ron Shelton, for MGM studios, 1988.

42 Michael Novak, *Belief and Unbelief* (New Brunswick, N.J.: Transaction, 2006), 135.

43: Stephen Colbert, from the television program *The Colbert Report*. See, for example, "Truthiness," October 17, 2005, at www.comedycentral.com/colbertreport/videos.jhtml?videoId=24039.

45: Georges Rey, in *Philosophers without God*, ed. Louise Anthony (New York: Oxford University Press, 2007), 244.

46: George MacDonald, *Thomas Wingfold, Curate* (Eureka, Calif.: Sunrise, 1988), 31.

49: See the chapter on good faith in André Comte-Sponville, *A Short Treatise on Great Virtues* (London: Vintage, 2003), 196ff.

51: Elton Trueblood, *A Place to Stand* (New York: Harper & Row, 1969), 39.

52: Frederick Buechner, *Wishful Thinking* (New York: Harper & Row, 1973), 3.

Chapter 4. Longing for Home

55: Hugh Walpole, quoted in Harry Emerson Fosdick, *Dear Mr. Brown: Letters to a Person Perplexed about Religion* (New York: Harper & Brothers, 1961), chap. 4.

56: On football and baseball, adapted from George Carlin, *Brain Droppings* (New York: Hyperion, 1998), 50–52.

56: Joe Kraus, "There's No Place Like Home," in *Baseball and Philosophy*, ed. Eric Bronson (New York: Open Court, 2004), 14ff.

56: Edgar Guest, "Home," in *101 Famous Poems* (Chicago: Contemporary Books, 1958), 152–53.

57: Stuart Kauffman, *At Home in the Universe: The Search for the Laws of Self-Organization and Complexity* (New York: Oxford University Press, 1995), 4.

58: Robert Frost, "The Death of the Hired Man."

58: A. J. Jacobs, *The Year of Living Biblically* (New York: Simon & Schuster, 2007), 60.

59: Augustine, *The Literal Meaning of Genesis*, Vol. 1:41, Ancient Christian Writers (New York: Newman Press, 1982).

59: Richard Swinbourne, *Is There a God?* (New York: Oxford University Press, 1996), 48–49.

59: Marilynne Robinson, *Gilead* (New York: Farrar, Straus and Giroux, 2004), 53.

61: Richard Foster, *Streams of Living Water* (San Francisco: HarperSanFrancisco, 1998), 171.

61: E. Edson and E. Savage-Smith, *Medieval Views of the Cosmos*. The Bodleian Library (New York: Oxford University Press, 2004), 9.

62: Sigmund Freud, cited in Bronson, *Baseball and Philosophy*, 12.

63: Lucretius, *On the Nature of the Universe*, introduction by John Godwin (New York: Penguin Classics, 2005), xvi.

65: Ray Vander Laan, *The Life and Ministry of the Messiah* (Grand Rapids: Zondervan, 1999), 150.

Chapter 5. The Leap

67: Nicholas Wolterstorff, *Lament for a Son* (Grand Rapids: Eerdmans, 1987), 76.

68: Fyodor Dostoyevsky, *The Possessed*, quoted in Philip Yancey, *Rumors of Another World: What on Earth Are We Missing?* (Grand Rapids: Zondervan, 2003), 34.

69: Alvin Plantinga, *Warranted Christian Belief* (New York: Oxford University Press, 2000), 174–75.

69: Thomas Aquinas, quoted in Frederick Buechner, *Listening to Your Life* (New York: HarperCollins, 1992), 273.

70: James Conner, *Pascal's Wager* (New York: HarperCollins, 2006), 143ff.

73: C. Stephen Evans, *Søren Kierkegaard's Christian Psychology* (Grand Rapids: Zondervan, 1990), 59ff.

74: Mortimer Adler, cited in *Philosophers Who Believe*, ed. Kelly James Clark (Downers Grove, Ill.: InterVarsity Press, 1993), 214.

75: Philip Yancey, *Finding God in Unexpected Places* (Nashville: Moorings, 1995), 171ff.

76: Yemelian Yaroslavsky, quoted in Brian Moynahan, *The Faith* (New York: Doubleday, 2002), viii.

78: For the account of the tormented son, see Matthew 17:14–21; Mark 9:14–32; and Luke 9:37–43.

81: Bruce Thielemann, unpublished sermon.

Chapter 6. Everybody Hopes

83: C. S. Lewis, quoted in Armand Nicholi, *The Question of God* (New York: Free Press, 2002), 46.

84: William Lad Sessions, *The Concept of Faith* (Ithaca, N.Y.: Cornell University Press, 1994), 197.

87: Sigmund Freud, *The Future of an Illusion* (London: Hogarth, 1962).

88: Paul Vitz, *Faith of the Fatherless* (Dallas: Spence, 1999).

88: Frederick Buechner, *Wishful Thinking* (New York: Harper & Row, 1973), 33–34.

94: Tom Wright: personal communication.

Chapter 7. The Strange Silence of God

99: Kenneth A. Taylor, in *Philosophers without God*, ed. Louise Anthony (New York: Oxford University Press, 2007), 244.

101: Jerome Frank, *Persuasion and Healing* (New York: Schocken, 1974).

103: Gary Parker, *The Gift of Doubt* (New York: Harper & Row, 1990), 62.

105: Bertrand Russell: source unknown.

105: Woody Allen, quoted in www.great-quotes.com/cgi-bin/author.cgi?letter=A.

105: Norwood Russell Hanson, "What I Do Not Believe," essay quoted in Lee Strobel, *The Case for Faith* (Grand Rapids: Zondervan, 2000), 254; emphasis added by Strobel.

107: Mother Teresa, *Come Be My Light*, ed. Brian Kolodiejchuk (New York: Doubleday, 2007), 104ff.

107: Christopher Hitchens, quoted in David Van Biema, "Mother Teresa's Crisis of Faith," in *Time* (August 23, 2007), 45.

107: Richard Dawkins, *The God Delusion* (New York: Houghton Mifflin, 2006), 292.

108: "Never doubt ," a quote from V. Raymond Edman, former Wheaton College president.

109: Robert Nozick, *Philosophical Explanations* (Cambridge, Mass.: Harvard University Press, 1981), 4.

110: Sam Harris, *Letter to a Christian Nation* (New York: Knopf, 2006), and *The End of Faith: Religion, Terror, and the Future of Reason* (New York: W. W. Norton, 2004).

111: Steven Weinberg, quoted in "Why We Are Here: The Great Debate," *International Herald Tribune* (April 26, 1999).

111: Cambodian massacre, cited in Dinesh D'Souza, "What's So Great about Christianity?" unpublished manuscript, chap. 19.

111: Elie Wiesel, from a dialogue with Antonio Monda quoted in Monda's book *Do You Believe?* (New York: Vintage, 2007), 172.

112: David Kinnaman, *Unchristian* (Grand Rapids: Baker, 2007), 26.

112: Frederick Buechner, *Listening to Your Life* (San Francisco: HarperSanFrancisco, 1992), 187.

112: Evelyn Waugh: source unknown.

113: Sigmund Freud, quoted in Armand Nicholi, *The Question of God* (New York: Free Press, 2002), 64.

113: Weinberg, quoted in "Why We Are Here: The Great Debate."

114: Jennifer Hecht, *Doubt: A History: The Great Doubters and Their Legacy of Innovation from Socrates and Jesus to Thomas Jefferson and Emily Dickinson* (New York: HarperCollins, 2003), 10.

115: Nicholas Wolterstorff, *Philosophers Who Believe: The Spiritual Journeys of Eleven Leading Thinkers* (Downers Grove, Ill.: InterVarsity Press, 1993), 274.

Chapter 8. When Doubt Goes Bad

119: Ernest Hemingway, quoted in Alister McGrath, *Doubting* (Downers Grove, Ill.: InterVarsity Press, 2006), 60.

121: Bart Ehrman, *Misquoting Jesus* (San Francisco: HarperSanFrancisco, 2005).

125: Glenn Most, *Doubting Thomas* (Cambridge: Harvard University Press, 2005), 80ff.

126: Os Guinness, *In Two Minds: The Dilemma of Doubt and How to Resolve It* (Downers Grove, Ill.: InterVarsity Press, 1976), 25.

126: Blaise Pascal, quoted in James Crenshaw, *Old Testament Wisdom* (Louisville: Westminster John Knox, 1998), 185.

128: Edward Gibbon, *The Decline and Fall of the Roman Empire* (New York: Heritage, 1946), 1776:1.22.

128: I am indebted to Pastor Scott Scruggs for this insight into Pilate and cynicism.

129: Jennifer Hecht, *Doubt: A History: The Great Doubters and Their Legacy of Innovation from Socrates and Jesus to Thomas Jefferson and Emily Dickinson* (New York: HarperCollins, 2003), 32.

130: Edward Ruffin, quoted in Oliver Burton, *The Age of Lincoln* (New York: Hill and Wang, 2007), 192.

130: C. S. Lewis, quoted in Armand Nicholi, *The Question of God* (New York: Free Press, 2002), 46.

132: G. K. Chesterton, quoted in Christopher Hitchens, *God Is Not Great: How Religion Poisons Everything* (New York: Twelve, 2007), 184.

132: Thomas Nagel, *The Last Word* (New York: Oxford University Press, 1997), 130.

132: Quoted in Nicholi, *Question of God*, 38.

132: Sigmund Freud, *Totem and Taboo* (London: Hogarth, 1962).

133: Czeslaw Milosz, quoted in Dinesh D'Souza, "What's So Great about Christianity?" unpublished manuscript, chap. 23.

Chapter 9. The Gift of Uncertainty

135: Frederick Buechner, *Wishful Thinking* (New York: Harper & Row, 1973), 26.

137: André Comte-Sponville, *A Short Treatise on the Great Virtues* (New York: Vintage, 2001), 223ff.

141: George MacDonald, *Thomas Wingfold, Curate* (Eureka, Calif.: Sunrise, 1988), 429–30.

142: Susan B. Anthony, quoted in Barbara Taylor, *Leaving Church* (San Francisco: HarperSanFrancisco, 2006), 7.

143: Mr. Dooley: cited in Antonio Monda, *Do You Believe?* (New York: Vintage, 2007), 145. Mr. Dooley is a character created by Irish satirist Finley Peter Dunne in 1898.

143: Xenophanes, quoted in Jennifer Hecht, *Doubt: A History: The Great Doubters and Their Legacy of Innovation from Socrates and Jesus to Thomas Jefferson and Emily Dickinson* (New York: HarperCollins, 2003), 7.

143: *Talladega Nights: The Ballad of Ricky Bobby*, movie, produced by Will Ferrell, Judd Apatow, and Jimmy Miller; directed by Adam McKay; written by Adam McKay and Will Ferrell; distributed by Columbia Pictures, 2006.

143: Buechner, *Wishful Thinking*, 190.

145: Joan Didion, *The Year of Magical Thinking* (New York: Knopf, 2005), 149.

147: "preferred comfort": cited in Louise Anthony, ed., *Philosophers without Gods* (New York: Oxford University Press, 2007), 73.

147: Richard Swinburne, *Is There a God?* (New York: Oxford University Press, 1996), 5.

147: Lewis Carroll, *Alice in Wonderland* (Philadelphia: Winston, 1957), 190.

148: Dallas Willard, quoted in Raphael Erwin McManus, *Soul Cravings* (Nashville: Nelson, 2006), entry 15.

148: C. S. Lewis, *Broadcast Talks* (London: Centenary, 1942), book 5, chap. 1, p. 33.

Chapter 10. Why I Believe

151: George MacDonald, *Thomas Wingfold, Curate* (Eureka, Calif.: Sunrise Books, 1988), 31.

152: G. K. Chesterton, *Orthodoxy* (New York: Doubleday, 1959), 180.

153: Alvin Plantinga, *Warrant, the Current Debate* (New York: Oxford University Press, 1993).

153: C. S. Lewis, *Mere Christianity* (Westwood, N.J.: Barbour and Co., 1952), chap. 1.
155: Dinesh D'Souza, "What's So Great about Christianity," unpublished manuscript, chap. 15.
159: This story was told to me by Mark Nelson, who is a friend of mine and a professor of philosophy at Westmont College and knows more than any one human being has a right to know.
161: Chesterton, *Orthodoxy*, 166–67.
161: Blaise Pascal, *Pensées*, trans. A. J. Krailsheimer (New York: Penguin, 1966), 64.
161: Steve Pinker, *The Blank Slate* (New York: Viking, 2002), 41ff.
162: "beyond ourselves": My friend Mark Nelson pointed out to me that philosopher Robert Nozick actually poses a thought experiment about an "experience machine" very much along these lines and comes to a similar conclusion that what we want is not just pleasant experiences, but to actually contact and live in reality beyond our own pleasant thoughts and feelings. See Robert Nozick, *Anarchy, State, and Utopia* (New York: Basic Books, 1974).
166: Elton Trueblood, *A Place to Stand* (New York: Harper & Row, 1969), 38.
166: MacDonald, *Thomas Wingfold, Curate*, 233.
167: Lee Strobel, *The Case for Faith* (Grand Rapids: Zondervan, 2000), 256–58.

Chapter 11. The Catcher

169: John Baillie, *A Reasoned Faith* (New York: Charles Scribner's Sons, 1963), 118.
172: Ben Patterson, chapel message, Westmont College, August 23, 2007.
175: Jean-Paul Sartre, cited in Frederick Buechner, *Wishful Thinking* (New York: Harper & Row, 1973), 3.
175: Jean-Paul Sartre, *The Words* (New York: George Brailler, 1954), 253.
176: Frederick Dale Bruner, *The Churchbook: Matthew 13–28*, Matthew: A Commentary (Grand Rapids: Eerdmans, 2005), 456.

When the Game Is Over, It All Goes Back in the Box

John Ortberg

Remember the thrill of winning at check-ers or Parcheesi? You become the Master of the Board – the victor over everyone else. But what happens after that? asks bestselling author John Ortberg. You know the answer: It all goes back in the box. You don't get to keep one token, one chip, one game card. In the end, the spoils of the game add up to nothing.

Using popular games as a metaphor for our temporal lives, *When the Game Is Over, It All Goes Back in the Box* neatly sorts out what's fleeting and what's permanent in God's kingdom. Being Master of the Board is not the point; being rich toward God is. Winning the game of life on Earth is a temporary victory; loving God and other people with all our hearts is an eternal one. Using humor, terrific stories, and a focus on winning "the right trophies," Ortberg paints a vivid picture of the priorities that all Christians will want to embrace.

Hardcover, Jacketed 978-0-310-25350-1

When the Game Is Over, It All Goes Back in the Box
Six Sessions on Living Life in the Light of Eternity

John Ortberg with Stephen and Amanda Sorenson

In the six sessions you will learn how to:

- Live passionately and boldly
- Learn how to be active players in the game that pleases God
- Find your true mission and offer your best
- Fill each square on the board with what matters most
- Seek the richness of being instead of the richness of having

DVD-ROM 978-0-310-28247-1
Participant's Guide 978-0-310-28246-4

If You Want to Walk on Water, You've Got to Get Out of the Boat

John Ortberg

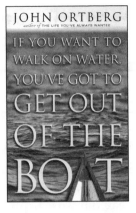

Deep within you lies the same faith and longing that sent Peter walking across the wind-swept Sea of Galilee toward Jesus.

John Ortberg invites you to consider the incredible potential that awaits you outside your comfort zone. Out on the risky waters of faith, Jesus is waiting to meet you in ways that will change you forever, deepening your character and your trust in God. The experience is terrifying. It's thrilling beyond belief. It's everything you'd expect of someone worthy to be called Lord.

The choice is yours to know him as only a water-walker can, aligning yourself with God's purpose for your life in the process. There's just one requirement: *If You Want to Walk on Water, You've Got to Get Out of the Boat.*

Hardcover, Jacketed 978-0-310-22863-9

If You Want to Walk on Water, You've Got to Get Out of the Boat

A 6-Session Journey on Learning to Trust God

John Ortberg with Stephen and Amanda Sorenson

If You Want to Walk on Water, You've Got to Get Out of the Boat kit includes:

- 90-minute VHS & DVD—use either format
- Leader's guide*
- Participant's guide*
- If You Want to Walk on Water, You've Got to Get Out of the Boat hardcover book*

Curriculum Kit 978-0-310-25053-1

DVD 978-0-310-26180-3

Leader's Guide 978-0-310-25055-5

*Also sold separately

God Is Closer Than You Think

This Can Be the Greatest Moment of Your Life Because This Moment Is the Place Where You Can Meet God

John Ortberg

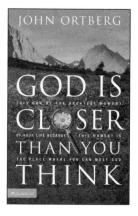

Intimacy with God can happen right now if you want it. A closeness you can feel, a goodness you can taste, a reality you can experience for yourself. That's what the Bible promises, so why settle for less? God is closer than you think, and connecting with him isn't for monks and ascetics. It's for business people, high school students, busy moms, single men, single women ... and most important, it's for YOU.

God Is Closer Than You Think shows how you can enjoy a vibrant, moment-by-moment relationship with your heavenly Father. Bestselling author John Ortberg reveals the face of God waiting to be discovered in the complex mosaic of your life. He shows you God's hand stretching toward you. And, with his gift for storytelling, Ortberg illustrates the ways you can reach toward God and complete the connection—to your joy and his.

Hardcover, Jacketed 978-0-310-25349-5

God Is Closer Than You Think

John Ortberg with Stephen and Amanda Sorenson

The Kit includes a six-session small group participant's guide, a six-session DVD (with a thirty-two-page leader's guide) featuring John Ortberg teaching, a CD-ROM (with sermon resources and promotional materials), and one copy of the hardcover book. The participant's guide, Small Group Edition DVD, and book are also sold separately.

Curriculum Kit 978-0-310-26635-8

WILLOW
Willow Creek Association

Willow Creek Association
Vision, Training, Resources for Prevailing Churches

This resource was created to serve you and to help you build a local church that prevails. It is just one of many ministry tools that are part of the Willow Creek Resources® line, published by the Willow Creek Association together with Zondervan.

The Willow Creek Association (WCA) was created in 1992 to serve a rapidly growing number of churches from across the denominational spectrum that are committed to helping unchurched people become fully devoted followers of Christ. Membership in the WCA now numbers over 12,000 Member Churches worldwide from more than ninety denominations.

The Willow Creek Association links like-minded Christian leaders with each other and with strategic vision, training, and resources in order to help them build prevailing churches designed to reach their redemptive potential. Here are some of the ways the WCA does that.

- **The Leadership Summit**—a once a year, two-and-a-half-day conference to envision and equip Christians with leadership gifts and responsibilities. Presented live at Willow Creek as well as via satellite broadcast to over 130 locations across North America, this event is designed to increase the leadership effectiveness of pastors, ministry staff, volunteer church leaders, and Christians in the marketplace.

- **Ministry-Specific Conferences** — throughout each year the WCA hosts a variety of conferences and training events — both at Willow Creek's main campus and offsite, across the U.S., and around the world — targeting church leaders and volunteers in ministry-specific areas such as: small groups, preaching and teaching, the arts, children, students, volunteers, stewardship, etc.

- **Willow Creek Resources®** — provides churches with trusted and field-tested ministry resources in such areas as leadership, evangelism, spiritual formation, spiritual gifts, small groups, stewardship, student ministry, children's ministry, the use of the arts — drama, media, contemporary music — and more.

- **WCA Member Benefits** — includes substantial discounts to WCA training events, a 20 percent discount on all Willow Creek Resources®, *Defining Moments* monthly audio journal for leaders, quarterly *Willow* magazine, access to a Members-Only section on WillowNet, monthly communications, and more. Member Churches also receive special discounts and premier services through WCA's growing number of ministry partners — Select Service Providers — and save an average of $500 annually depending on the level of engagement.

For specific information about WCA conferences, resources, membership, and other ministry services contact:

Willow Creek Association
P.O. Box 3188
Barrington, IL 60011-3188
Phone: 847-570-9812
Fax: 847-765-5046
www.willowcreek.com

Share Your Thoughts

With the Author: Your comments will be forwarded to the author when you send them to *zauthor@zondervan.com*.

With Zondervan: Submit your review of this book by writing to *zreview@zondervan.com*.

Free Online Resources at
www.zondervan.com/hello

 Zondervan AuthorTracker: Be notified whenever your favorite authors publish new books, go on tour, or post an update about what's happening in their lives.

 Daily Bible Verses and Devotions: Enrich your life with daily Bible verses or devotions that help you start every morning focused on God.

 Free Email Publications: Sign up for newsletters on fiction, Christian living, church ministry, parenting, and more.

 Zondervan Bible Search: Find and compare Bible passages in a variety of translations at www.zondervanbiblesearch.com.

 Other Benefits: Register yourself to receive online benefits like coupons and special offers, or to participate in research.

HILLSBORO PUBLIC LIBRARIES
Hillsboro, OR
Member of Washington County
COOPERATIVE LIBRARY SERVICES